Lionel Stock

The Mother Church Your Mother Never Told You Of

Also by Gavin White and published by SCM Press

How the Churches Got to Be the Way they Are

Gavin White

The Mother Church Your Mother Never Told You Of

SCM PRESS

ISBN 0 334 01042 X

First published 1993 by
SCM Press Ltd
26–30 Tottenham Road London N1 4BZ

Typeset by Regent Typesetting, London
Printed in Great Britain by
Mackays of Chatham, Kent

Contents

1

Beginnings

As we all know, or as Einstein has told us, time is relative – we are only able to measure one thing in time against another. And our view of time is relative; no two human beings could agree on how long it took for an hour to pass, let alone a year (unless there were climatic changes) or a millennium. In studying early church history, there are two extremes. Briefly, conservatives believe that 'long ago' was only yesterday, and liberals that it was so far back that the people involved were barely human. The conservative view leads to the assumption that we can quite simply put ourselves in the place of the early Christians and think as they thought and do as they did. Some will even say that they have 'got back to' such and such a book of the New Testament, and are re-living the experiences of that book. Nothing much happened between the writing of the New Testament and a series of modern calamities beginning with Darwin or Freud.

Liberals take the opposite view. Time has gone so slowly. So much has happened since the days of the apostolic church that we are barely able to make guesses as to what the evidence means, or what it was to be a Christian in those days. Everything is changed. Even if we did know what had happened, it would not be much use to us since we are so utterly different from the early Christians. The evidence must be entirely re-interpreted, and the words of the apostles or the fathers re-written to show what they would have said if they had been like us. For they were primitive, and all that has come to us from their time is itself primitive and must be made new.

If this radical difference in perspective were not enough to confuse the whole subject, there is another difference, or perhaps the same difference seen in a different way. This is that the universe was either created all of a go, in six days or less, or was evolved gradually over the ages. Of course this lies at the heart of the Darwinian controversy, in so far as there still is such a thing, but it is far wider than that. If it was a once-and-for-all creation, with God not doing much since, then we may presume that the universe was perfect, or at least complete, when handed over to Adam according to contract. And we may also presume that the Bible was perfect, or at least complete, at an early stage. There was no working out of the meaning of it to be done in subsequent generations and centuries. It was there, it was adequate, what more could anyone want?

And, to take the argument a little further, human beings as they are now have been so in the mind of God and have been so from the beginning. Skin colour could not have developed in subsequent ages – for all practical purposes there really were no subsequent ages. It is no accident that the 'Princeton theology' of literal inerrancy in scripture came from the seminary which served the Old School Presbyterians of the United States who were divided from the New School by their acceptance of slavery. Again, gender is seen in the same way – it was there in the beginning, and as it was then, so it is now, and so it will always be. What is now was in the mind of God and was determined from the very beginning.

Of course the once-for-all creation was generally believed in the eighteenth century, and the gradual continuing creation was generally believed in the nineteenth century, and we in the twentieth have inherited a mixture of the two. But if we believe in a single creation period, then anything thereafter is pollution. It should be scraped off. You have only to prove that something developed in the second century, or the third, or the fourth, or last Thursday, and it is not of the real church. The real church was as it was delivered by the manufacturer, and before it was driven off.

This leads to the assumption that the early Christians were much better Christians than the Christians of today. The evidence, and there is a good deal of it, is that they were a pretty scruffy lot. (In fact the Creed should be altered to say, 'I believe in one Holy, Catholic, Apostolic, and Scruffy Church'. But I wouldn't sit up all night waiting for this to happen.) Yet if the early Christians were a scruffy lot, this is hardly surprising. Had the early Christians all been super-Christians, then the Christian faith would have been only suitable for such people as scarcely exist in the real world.

To assume that the early Christians were wonderful supposes that Christianity had a sell-by date, and its effectiveness became weaker with every generation. It is in something of this spirit that certain Westerners become intrigued by the Eastern Orthodox, not as real Christians living real lives in the modern world, but as if they were survivals of the apostolic age, untouched by history, like that fish long believed to be extinct but found in the nets of a Malagasy fisherman and, had it not been eaten, very disturbing to the palaeontologists.

Of course the idea that the early Christians were wonderful has been re-inforced by the recent popularity of what is called 'resurrection faith'. A contrast has been made between a group of befuddled disciples and those who, after the resurrection, were suddenly capable of everything. What lay behind this was the failure of scholars to 'prove' the resurrection in an age that demanded proof of everything. Since the New Testament could not prove the resurrection to universal satisfaction, it was pointed out that it did prove the faith of the disciples after the resurrection. From this it could be assumed that the resurrection did happen. Of course this is putting a subtle and respectable argument very crudely, but the result was to interpret all evidence to suggest that the disciples before the resurrection were awful and after the resurrection were wonderful. Nowadays the problem of whether the New Testament proves the resurrection has faded into the background, together with a world in which everything needs proof, but the emphasis on the faith of the disciples after the resurrection remains. The result has been a generation of preachers who tell their huddled congregations that if they had real resurrection faith they would not only convert the neighbourhood but even pay for a new heating system. We should treat such teaching with caution, and look at what the New Testament actually says about the early Christians.

But this brings us on to the question of whether the early church ever had any faith but the one it has now, and whether there is a pure faith which once existed but no longer does. We are told that the church has, throughout history, mixed up the Christian faith and the customs of the society in which it has lived. It has successively been identified with the philosophy and the structures of the Roman empire, the Byzantine empire, the Carolingian empire, the British empire, and any other empire which may have existed or may even exist today. Missionaries are blamed for having gone to other lands and having taken their cultural baggage with them; if we could strip off the husk of secularity, we would find pure Christianity underneath, as if we were dealing with coconuts. And yet this is just another way of saying that long ago was last Thursday; in the Christian faith there can be or should be no history – the faith comes down unchanged and unchanging.

Of course there may be religions in which this is held to be possible; in some ways Islam approximates to this ideal, with a divine revelation which can never be so much as translated into another language. But a religion which locates the divinity in human flesh involves it in history, and Christianity cannot exist in a test-tube. There is no pure essence of Christianity. A religion of God-made-flesh means that the forms of Jewish life and Roman empire are going to be carried round the world. There is no other way in which Christianity could travel without ceasing to be Christianity. Of course added to the Jewish life and Roman empire will be double entry book-keeping and priests holding their hands in certain ways and a miscellaneous collection of hymn-tunes, but these are the husk without which there would be no coconut. Christianity does not push its way through history, it carries history with it.

And it is equally false to believe that we can ignore the history on the one hand, or say it is 'just history' on the other. History is given, and it is neither an obstruction nor a substitute. There can be no Christianity without it, but it is not Christianity in itself. And, like the husk on the coconut, it comes in layers. It is much too simple to suggest that there are only two points of time involved – our own and that of the early church. What we have from the early church has been filtered down to us through the ages. We have to take account of how it has been re-worked and developed, or debased and corrupted, by the scholars who have handled it in any particular century, or perhaps in several different centuries. Did they add new layers of husk, or did they confuse the picture by removing too much?

Some years ago the American historian E.R. Hardy was asked to study the question of women leaders in non-Christian religions of apostolic times with a view to showing how this might relate to the ordination of women. He found that women did not lead in such religions, and concluded that the early Christians did not ordain women as it never occurred to them to do so.

This allowed his readers to believe what they liked, and on such a subject they were sure to do this anyway. Some would say that if it never occurred to the early Christians to ordain women, then the thing was unthinkable. Otherwise, they would have thought about it. Clearly the Holy Spirit led them not to think about it, and that is all we need to know. Others would say that if the early Christians had thought about it and had reached certain conclusions, then those conclusions would be worth taking seriously. But if they had never thought about it then what they did, or did not do, was not binding and could be set aside.

Behind this difference lies another difference, and that is how Christians see the Holy Spirit at work. Is the process to be likened to an override in a nuclear power station which tells an operator that his action would contaminate a continent so it is cancelled and that is that? Does it prevent thinking, or does it inspire thinking? Does it override the operator or does it guide the operator? The answer to this question must depend on yet another question – how corrupt are our minds? If they are so corrupt that they will mislead us and contaminate continents every day of the week, then anything which cuts our mental processes out of the real business of life is to be welcomed. If, on the other hand, they are not very seriously corrupted, then they should be used. And if they have not been used on any particular subject, then that subject is wide open for investigation.

In reading of the early church, we shall find both these extremes. There will be those who determine what was done, and then assume that it is the duty of all subsequent generations of Christians to do the same. There will also be those who determine what was done and then determine that it was done because the early Christians were primitive people who had not the educational advantages available to us, so it is of no account. Happily, most study of the early church falls somewhere near the middle, and if it does not, then we can identify the thinking behind it. And we can treat it with due caution.

But can we know anything at all about the early church? In so far as we can know anything about anything we can know about this. We may change the meaning or weight of the evidence merely by thinking about it, and others may have passed down to us changed meanings of previous generations, but this is true in all aspects of life. We do have a great deal of evidence, and we can make as much sense of it as we can of any other evidence.

First, there is the New Testament. It is common to regard this as a sort of architect's drawing on the basis of which the church began. In fact it is more a record of what the church wrote once it had begun. The epistles could not have been written to churches which did not exist. The Apocalypse (Revelation) could not have complained of churches which did not exist. The Gospels are less obviously linked to the early church; that they were read in small bits in church on Sundays did not mean that they were written solely or even mainly for that purpose. But there is really no end to the New Testament. It does not stop with a clear line drawn between what is in and what is out. It ends in a mixture of documents once given authority, or hovering on the verge of being scripture. Some made it, while others did not. And those that did not get recognized as scripture merge into the vast collection which we call the Fathers of the Church, or Patristic writings. It was said of Origen that nobody could ever read all that he had written. Fortunately the others wrote somewhat less, but the recent discovery of some letters of Augustine, which had been quietly sitting for centuries in a collection of Augustine's works in a centre devoted to studying nothing but Augustine, will give some idea of the sheer mass of the treasures of the past which have come down to us.

Nor is that all. The non-Christian observers of early days may have been few, but they did exist. There is a fascinating exchange of letters from as early as 112 in which the governor of Bithynia, Pliny the Younger, asked the Emperor Trajan what to do with Christians. He gave details of the sect which would be less horrific if we were not told that he had inflicted torture on deaconesses to obtain those details. These letters will strike a familiar note with anyone who has ever dealt with a government department. But while persecutors kept a careful record of questions and answers to justify their promotions, there were also pagan philosophers who wrote elaborate arguments against Christianity.

Then there are the diggings of the archaeologists. These must be treated with caution, and not because, as the old saying goes, 'they dig the ancient rubbish up and then they write it down'. It is more tricky than that. If archaeologists find remains, those have remained because they were more solid than normal, and thus they are abnormal, unless they were preserved by a landfall or some other chance feature. Then there is the tendency for discoveries to be welcomed if they prove a theory, or ignored if they do not. And they are always welcomed if romantic. In 1802 three tiles were dug up near Rome, reading LUMENA/PAX TE/CUM FI, which could mean, 'Light and peace to you, with Faith'. But the tiles were re-arranged to read, 'Pax Tecum Filumena', or 'Peace be with you Philomena'. Nearby bones and a jug which had once contained what might have been blood led to a devotion to a virgin martyr. It was later doubted if the tiles were connected with the bones or with the jug, and in 1961 the whole devotion to St Philomena was abolished by Rome, to the great embarrassment of an American bishop who was to dedicate a new church to that saint on the following day. He dedicated it to the Precious Blood instead.

So we have the New Testament and the writings of the Fathers and the diggings of the archaeologists and the work of church historians from Eusebius of Caesaria in the fourth century until the latest book just off the press. We have interpretations and re-interpretations and attempts to skin the history alive to get at the real meaning, and attempts to skin-graft it back to where it was before it was skinned alive. We have indexes and chronographies and computer databases. But we still have to think about it.

Finally, just as there is no way of insulating the essence of Christianity from history, there is no way of insulating it from ourselves. We change it as we study it, and it also changes us – though this is something which we would often prefer not to acknowledge. We are supposed to be the impartial observers, but in fact we are not.

There is a science-fiction story of a human space-traveller who crashed on a remote planet. After crawling across a desert under a blazing sun, or several blazing suns, the traveller reached a building in which was a shower-head and a pedal. Pressing the pedal produced, not water, but a caustic substance. Eventually the mechanism managed to produce a few drops of water, but the effort cracked the walls, and the traveller lay down to die. Awakening hours later, and pressing the pedal, the traveller found the mechanism had made the correct adjustment, and joyfully lapped up the substance from the shower-head with a green forked tongue, while swivelling all four eyes to the corners of the building, and playfully striking the floor with a long flat tail. The student of church history may not end up with a green tongue or four eyes or a long tail, though stranger things have happened to some students of this subject. But the student will change. That is what church history does to you.

2

Gnosticism

Gnosticism spread through the church of the second century like a computer virus. Masquerading as the real thing, it worked its way into churches all over the Mediterranean and proceeded to eat away at the Christian faith, doing untold damage until detected. It was then cast out into utter darkness from which it was only brought back by nineteenth-century Liberal Protestants who thought it was liberal, which it was not, and protestant, which it was not. It was flying saucer stuff.

Gnosticism (the G is silent, but nobody concerned with Gnosticism has ever been silent) was not a heresy, since it was not an exaggeration or a distortion of Christian doctrine. It was at least partly an outside body which had broken in and multiplied, at the expense of the churches on which it fed. Its origins have always been obscure, but it seems that it came from the East, perhaps from Persian Zoroastrianism, and was one of the many systems called dualist, believing in two gods instead of one, and believing that true religion was rejecting one god and affirming the other. Furthermore, it held that the one god who was evil had created the world, so that all that was material was evil. But this explanation of Gnosticism is only part of the story. It may be that no single explanation will cover Gnosticism, since Gnosticism was never one thing. It was a virus which invaded Christianity, but it was much more. It was a number of attempts by a young and inexperienced church to relate Christianity to various strands of life at that time. If we want to define it more closely, it was the sum of all the attempts which ultimately failed, while the other attempts came to be accepted as orthodoxy.

Mainstream Gnosticism was attractive to many Christians. As religions go, Christianity is difficult. The material world is made by God, and it is good, but then it has gone wrong, and if it is not bad, it is certainly flawed, and human nature was good, and then was flawed, and is getting back, thanks to Jesus Christ, to a state in which it will be as good as it was and perhaps much better. The Christian is called to be in the world but not of it, to flee the world and to save it. If this does correspond pretty closely to the mixture of good and evil which everyone meets in real life, it is not easy to grasp overnight, and the Christian faith requires a long process of growth. Readers of the *Hitchhiker's Guide to the Galaxy* books will remember a computer programmed to solve the great question of 'Life, the Universe, and Everything'. After many years it pronounced the answer to be forty-two. This is a multiple of seven and six; in the New Testament seven is perfection or good, and six is imperfection or bad, so forty-two is a multiple of both good and bad. It would be far easier to have six as the answer and consider the world to be simply bad, or even to have seven as the answer and consider the world to be simply good. Gnosticism took the answer to be six.

Furthermore, the faithful Christian who prepared with such hope and assurance for baptism may have been dismayed to find that after baptism there were still temptations, and life was harder rather than easier after agreeing to aim at a higher standard. And there are troughs as well as peaks in prayer and devotion. It is during one of the troughs, when all seems black, that the Christian is approached by the salesman for the product with the secret ingredient. Christianity really is easy, and it really does everything for you with little effort, and it is quite clear and simple. Instead of all this double-talk about the creation being good and then bad, it is quite simply bad, and was made by a very bad god, and should be avoided by Christians, who have no duty towards it. In fact they do not belong in this world at all; they were once happy souls floating around in the heavens until trapped in loathsome human bodies by sexual acts which are therefore evil. Gnosticism will give them the clues to find the road out of the material world.

Of course it may be argued by the Christian, despite the attractions of all this, that it is not found in the readings in church, and not found in the traditions of the church. The answer to this is easy; those closest to Christ knew that most people would not be worthy of the true knowledge (or 'gnosis' in Greek) and so they kept the true knowledge for the few who could appreciate it, while providing a surface religion for the rest. But *you* are clearly worthy of this true knowledge and have been selected – anyone who has received junk-mail telling them they have been chosen for a chance of a tropical cruise or a new car or an electronic toothbrush will be familiar with the technique.

There were many different sorts of Gnostics. The earliest are mentioned in the New Testament, notably in I Corinthians 6, in Colossians 2, and in I Timothy, though these are not always recognized by modern readers for what they are. The closest to standard Christianity was Marcion, who arrived in Rome around 140 and made gifts to the church which had to be returned when he was cast out and started Marcionite churches in various cities. He taught a 'God of love' who was good, and a 'god of law' who was bad, and who inspired the Old Testament, and put Jesus to death. To do this Marcion had to repudiate the Old Testament and all the New except part of Luke and a few epistles. In fact Marcion probably gained many followers who were troubled by elements of cruelty or injustice in the Old Testament, and who read all scriptures as if they were at the same level and to be used in the same way. Like all Gnostics, Marcion held that Christ could not have been born of a woman, since flesh is evil, so he only pretended to be human.

Valentinus lived at Rome from about 136 to 165, and had a system of 'pleroma' or a world of ideas, parallel to the world of things, and with Aeons, of whom one gave birth to the creator. Basileides of Alexandria is credited with this description of Christ. 'The light, therefore, which came down from the Ogdoad above to the son of the Hebdomad, descended from the Hebdomad upon Jesus the Son of Mary, and he was enlightened being

11

illuminated with the light that shone upon him.' But much of the teaching of Valentinus was derived from a rather simplified Platonic philosophy, which could well have been familiar to many in the ancient world, and much of all Gnosticism was derived from Eastern teachings which would have been even more familiar. The new sects allowed recent converts to keep their old convictions in a Christian form. But there is always a narrow line between keeping old convictions in a Christian form, and keeping new convictions in a non-Christian form, and some of those who did the first probably did so while trying to do the second.

Of course, the church fought back. J.A. Jungmann has shown how earlier worship avoided too much stress on sacrifice since the main threat to Christianity was paganism, and there was a danger of converts thinking the sacrifice of the eucharistic sacrament was the same thing as killing animals in a temple. After paganism ceased to be so influential, and Gnosticism became a threat, the altar ceased to be a simple table and became elaborate, and was actually called an altar. The offering of bread and wine was done with ceremony so that no Gnostic could pretend that the church thought bread and wine to be evil and unworthy of being offered to God. In the main prayer of the eucharist were the words, 'Therefore with angels and archangels, and with all the company of heaven, we laud and magnify thy holy name …' Why mention the angels here? To show that, whatever they are, they must be worshipping the one God, for Gnostics had elaborate lists of angels who were over God or equal to him. The same tactics led to the words of the hymn *Te Deum*. 'To thee all angels cry aloud, the heavens and all the powers therein. To thee cherubim and seraphim continually do cry …' No Christian denomination has ever defined what a seraph may be, but if there is such a being it must be held to worship the one God.

But there were other means of defence. The Gnostics claimed to have the true knowledge, and it was easy enough to show that the churches had a direct link to the apostles or those who had known them, while the Gnostics had none. On the scriptures, the Gnostics were obliged to produce their own, naming them for apostles in many cases; this may seem very wicked until we remember that many books of the New Testament are honoured with the name of an apostle when it is almost certain they were not written by that person. But this led to some confusion as earnest Christians listened to what at first seemed to be good Christian teaching but on reflection turned out to be something of a cuckoo in the nest. One example is the 'Gospel of St Thomas', dug up in Egypt in 1945, which had bits out of the present New Testament, and a few bits which could be true memories of Jesus Christ, and other parts which were clearly Gnostic. 'These are the secret words which the living Jesus spoke ... Whoever finds the explanation of these words will not taste death.' The words were secret, and it was the explanation of them which brought eternal life, not any action of Christ. 'Jesus said, when you see him who was not born of woman, prostrate yourselves upon your face and adore him, he is your father.' Here is the Gnostic horror of sex, and of being born of a woman, and it is no wonder that the church guarded against such teaching by details of the birth of Christ and honour given to his mother. 'Simon Peter said to them, let Mary go out from us because women are not worthy of the life. Jesus said, see, I shall lead her, so that I will make her male ... '

The answer to such writings was to establish a list of the authentic works of the early church, and by 150 this was largely accepted, though a few details remained to be tidied up later. But there was also the memory of who had been bishop in each city, from which it could be determined that the regular bishops had known those who knew the apostles, while the Gnostics had not.

And there came to be a considerable speculation on the soul. If the Gnostics claimed that souls were from heaven and did not really belong in bodies, then the souls would not fit bodies but would be spherical, on the grounds that that was the finest shape available. To this question Tertullian, a North African Christian who later embraced the Montanist faith, devoted much effort. He argued that the soul was both born and created, and he quoted a female mystic who saw a soul and observed it to be shaped like a human body, which showed it must belong in one. He further identified the soul with the breath of life in creation, as received by Adam, and Eve received her soul from Adam, but in all other cases the soul and body are conceived and born together. As a by-product of this teaching the souls of the newborn had to come from their father with no participation by the mother, and this did not help the church in considering questions of gender. Yet Tertullian's teaching on this subject was so close to that of the secular society of his day that this would probably have happened anyway. (There is a curious echo of all this in a poem of this century by Rupert Brooke, entitled *Thoughts on the Shape of the Human Body*. 'Fantastic shape to mazed fantastic shape, Straggling, irregular, perplexed, embossed, Grotesquely twined ... ' and so on, when it would be better to, 'Grow to a radiant round love, and bear, Unfluctuant passion for some perfect sphere ... ' Of course Brooke was writing about bodies and not souls, but the principle was the same.)

At this point attention must be directed to the Liberal Protestants, already mentioned. Their belief was, crudely and probably unfairly stated, and they were neither as stupid or as unorthodox as modern thinkers tend to assume, that humanity was not really very bad after all, and progress was making huge strides, and with a bit more education and bit more care there would be no more sin, or what passed for sin, and therefore there was no need of a saviour. Everything in the Gospels which suggested that Christ was Son of God must have been added later, and all the sacramental part was the work of a later priesthood. The real Christ was not the saviour on the cross but the Teacher of Galilee, and the creeds with their dogmatism overlooked the essential part of his ministry of teaching and healing which were signified by a single comma. The most distinguished scholar of this school was Adolf von Harnack, who would have been horrified by such a crude description of his teaching, for he inspired respect not only for his scholarship but for his devotion. But in the closing years of the last century the optimistic view of human nature was everywhere.

The trouble was that the teaching of the early church fathers and of the New Testament did not agree with that view. The early church had clearly believed that humanity needed saving, and that Christ was God and had come to save. But could it be that the early church as we knew it was not the real church? Was it really the work of a later generation of writers who had created a highly structured organization instead of the simple fellowships of earlier days? Had they then manufactured evidence to support the view that their organization went back to the apostles? The difficulty was that all evidence of the simple fellowships could not have been destroyed – but, they realized, it had not been destroyed, only distorted. The true early Christians had been the Gnostics, and if they did not seem to be simple fellowships of true believers, then this was because we only knew them from the descriptions of their enemies, men like Tertullian and Irenaeus, who had good cause to suppress the truth about the so-called Gnostics. And so there came to be a belief, usually unexamined and sometimes unconscious, that the Gnostics really had something to offer to all Christians which had been suppressed by a priesthood which desired to control this new movement and to exploit it, and to bind it in rules and dogma and thus to quench the spirit.

There was a sinister side to this. In those days anti-Semitism was at its height, and there was a general assumption that what was Jewish was worldly, and that there was a Jewish strain in the Christian church which must be kept under control if it could not be eliminated. And here were the Gnostics, of whom it was known that they had made a list of authorized books of the Bible, rejecting everything which was Jewish, and rejecting the God of the Old Testament, and rejecting what was material. If the merely academic enthusiasm for Gnosticism cannnot be blamed for anti-Semitism it gave it a certain respectability in Christian circles. In fact its respectability went beyond Christian circles; Simone Weil, who was herself agnostic Jewish but drawn to Christianity, was able to write, even after the Second World War, that 'Hebrew prejudices, which infiltrated into the very substance of Christianity, have uprooted Europe, cutting it off from its millennial past ... We might perhaps now say that the whole world is uprooted and widowed of its past, and that is so because the new-born Christianity did not know how to detach itself from a tradition which, after all, had ended up with

15

the murder of Christ.' And many a less thoughtful person would have agreed.

But the theory that Gnosticism had been distorted by its enemies could only be believed while the Gnostic writings were lost, save for odd scraps found in quotations from those determined to do them down. The whole situation changed radically when an Arab camel-driver came upon a treasure trove of Gnostic writings at Nag Hammadi in Upper Egypt in 1945. Although the camel-driver's mother used some of these writings for fuel, enough survived to show that Gnosticism had been what its enemies had always said it was. The ideas of the fellowships of believers with their simple faith in goodness as set forth by the Teacher of Galilee were swamped by the strings of passwords and names by which the initiates could gain control over heavenly beings, and be passed up the line from one to another.

But there is another belief about Gnosticism – that it had a respect for the feminine which was lacking in orthodox Christianity. But even some of those who promote this view agree that in Gnostic documents the male is to the female as the divine is to the human. And if the argument rests on the feminine names of certain Gnostic deities, we should look at the part they played in the Gnostic scheme of things. For most of them we do not know that they played any part, for only the name is given, but there is one of whom we know quite a bit, Sophia, the Greek name for Wisdom. And in Gnostic thought she was the one who yearned to see the Father, and her desire having become detached it became Sophia Achemoth who was expelled from heaven and led to the formation of this world. This is not very different from the myth of Adam and Eve in blaming it all on a woman, and we are left with the conclusion that any religion of that day took it for granted that women were inferior or cursed, and worked this into their system by an appropriate myth. The Gnostics were no exception. But there is a difference between Christianity and Gnosticism here, in that Christianity seems to have mistakenly soaked up a lot of the hostility to sex and hostility to women which were common in that era, while Gnosticism seems to have made that hostility basic to its system. As in so many other respects, Gnosticism which rejected the world was actually closer to the teachings of the world than was Christianity.

By the end of the second century Gnosticism was in retreat. It survived in odd patches throughout the ancient world, emerging in the Middle Ages as the cult of the Bogomils in the Balkans, and of the Cathari or Albigenses in France. There has been a good deal of speculation as to why it declined, with the emphasis being on the defensive works of Christian thinkers. Yet there is a much more likely reason why it faded. It did not work. It could not work. Like most simple systems which claim to get to the root of the matter and avoid complications, it did not get to the root of the matter and it did not avoid the complications. It was all very well to say that the world was evil and that we did not belong in it, but had been kidnapped from heaven. Yet the same people who at first welcomed this teaching had to live in a world which was clearly a mixture of what was good and what was bad. They needed a religion which was at least partly anchored in this world, and treasured material things. And the names of the elemental spirits of the universe, fascinating though they had been to puzzle out in the writings, did not do anything for those who knew them. The Gnostics were sometimes supposed to have been driven out of the church, and no doubt some were, but it seems much more likely that they returned to the battle with evil in the world amongst their fellow Christians and Gnosticism was heard of less and less.

This raises another question. Was Gnosticism really an alien body in the Christian church, or was it a necessary stage in the coming-of-age of Christianity? All too often it seems that the whole set of extraordinary names in extraordinary languages must have been totally alien, and it was just bad luck that it hit Christianity when it did. And yet Christianity has been shaped by the critical conflict with Gnosticism. Perhaps the developed doctrine of apostolic succession and the definition of what was scripture and what was not, and the balance between offertory and consecration in the liturgy, and the theology of Irenaeus, would in due course of time have emerged anyway. On the other hand, we can imagine a church without any of these things, and yet there is no such church. If these things were only needed to face a single oriental invasion, they would have withered when that danger passed, and they have not withered. We are therefore faced with the possibility that some form of Gnosticism was necessary for the growth of the church, even if it may have been more of a vaccination than a baby-food. The church needed Gnosticism in order to reject it.

And perhaps every Christian needs to pass through some sort of Gnostic phase in order to outgrow it. And there are modern Gnostics; not the small groups in California which seek to revive a religion based on ancient texts and white robes, but any number of groups which claim to have reduced everything to a few simple rules, and to have reduced life to a few simple rules, though it is made more interesting by measuring the sides of the Bermuda Triangle or the Great Pyramid and multiplying it by the number you first thought of. They do not last long, these groups, for ultimately they have the same drawbacks as Gnosticism of earlier days, and they do not work. But it may be that each Christian finds the real thing too difficult or too slow or too demanding, and goes for some alternative with the secret ingredient, and only when that fails, returns to the painful encounter with the real thing.

There used to be a theory that before birth a European child passed through all races of mankind while in the womb until born in the highest; those with Down's Syndrome were called Mongols at least partly because they were thought to have been born before their time, and if born even earlier would have been Africans or Australian Aborigines. Of course this is nonsense, as is the theory that children enjoy woodcraft as they are passing through the lives of North American Indians, but something like it may apply in Christian life.

3

Evangelism

Billy Graham visited Scotland in 1991. It was all very old-fashioned. There was a country singer, and an ex-commissioner of police, and Graham told a story of the bit of scripture he was using being a favourite with the Queen. None of these items would have made much impression upon the general public, but with thirty thousand church people bussed in from all over the country, it was right on target. In times of decline churches are like rock-pools left behind by the falling tide, and their cultural backwardness serves as a shield. Secular ideas cannot get at them.

In America Graham had been converted by the rabble-rouser Mordecai Ham, moved into the Fundamentalist rock-pool, then out towards the mainstream, taking most former Fundamentalists with him. (There is a hilarious article by the Jewish writer, Harry Gold, who chased Billy Graham around an Atlanta department store while he did his Christmas shopping, quizzing him on anti-Semitism. Billy Graham came up smelling of roses.) In the 1950s Scotland had been vital for Graham; he found that with ordinary church sponsorship he could draw a bigger crowd, and when he went on to New York he accepted sponsorship from mainstream Protestants. (Criticized for this by his former allies, he replied that Paul at Athens had accepted sponsorship from Epicureans and Stoics.) In fact he could do what he did in the 1950s as that was a period of church-increase, and when he took Christians out of their rock-pools they were more likely to influence their neighbours than be influenced by them. By 1991 it was to be a different story.

By taking Fundamentalists into the mainstream in the 1950s, Graham gave them new dignity. Their hymns and choruses, based on the 'Country and Western' style of the hill-state South, were taken across the world, and were regarded by the wider world as aspects of the better life lived in America. But there was a contradiction at the heart of this cultural transplant. While the wider world saw 'Country and Western' as successful because it was American, Americans saw it as unsuccessful because it was hill-state. Taking Fundamentalism back into the mainstream meant paying a cultural price in America itself, but outside America the Billy Graham campaign was sustained by a cultural subsidy.

In the 1991 rallies, the advertisements hinged on the question of whether life had meaning, which might well interest and attract outsiders. But Billy Graham did not mention this – he took for granted that life had meaning, and called for a response from those who were already convinced, or had been convinced but had fallen away. To the outsiders, and some must have managed to squeeze into the stadium between the massed ranks of churchgoers, his preaching cannot have meant very much. But he did give churchgoers an opportunity to go forward and re-commit themselves, or to commit themselves more deeply. But this was not really evangelism; it was revival of a faith already there.

None of which may seem to have much to do with the early church, and yet it has. There were times and places in which the church was growing a shell to protect itself from the pagan world, and there were times and places when the church was able to move out and change the pagan world. There were times and places when Christianity was carried on a wave of Roman culture, when that culture seemed modern and successful. There were times when it carried Roman culture even though that seemed neither modern nor successful. And there were times and places when it was carried by Eastern culture of one sort or another, and not by Roman culture at all. Finally, there were times when it was taught as a revival of something already believed, and times when it was taught as something new and startling. It was not a simple business of just preaching a simple gospel.

Then there were miracles. Or were there? If we believe that Christianity was strong at the beginning but got weaker as time passed, then we will believe that there were miracles in the early church which converted people. We will also believe that there are none today so we have to convince people with arguments. But the belief that the early church grew through miracles usually comes from believing that the early church existed a long time ago. It was quite unlike the church of today. On the other hand, those who believe that early Christianity spread as it gave a reasonable account of human existence are those who believe that the early church was like that of today.

But there is a paradox in this. Usually, as has been argued already, conservatives believe that the early church was like that of today, and liberals that it was totally alien. But conservatives tend to believe that conversion is by miracles, since they do not have a high view of the human mind or human anything else. And liberals tend to believe that people are reasonable, and miracles are not. So each group has an equal tendency to believe either side of the argument. Again, those who argue for conversion by miracles tend to assume that it is the power of miracles which matters, and not the type of miracles. If the ancient world really was one in which miracles were taken for granted, then what would have mattered would not have been so much the existence of miracles as their meaning. But was the ancient world really a world of miracles?

We tend to assume that the ancients could accept all sorts of unexplained events as miracles since they were not scientific. If this were true, it would mean that almost anything was a miracle, and thus there was nothing special in a miracle being a miracle. But it was not true. The ancients had a system of science which, if it was wildly wrong in some respects, served them well in most respects. How much room that system left for miracles varied then as it does now. We have recently moved from a very rigid view of science, in which everything was presumed to be determined, to what John Polkinghorne has called 'a world of intertwined order and novelty' or, in Popper's words, 'a world of clouds and clocks'. There were those in the first centuries of the Christian era who were strong on clocks, and those who were strong on clouds, and emphasis on miracle or on reasonable debate would be found accordingly.

So, how did the early church grow? Slowly. Estimates are only that, but by 250 barely two per cent of the population of the empire were Christian. They were to be found in the areas travelled by Paul, and in North Africa, and in the Rhone Valley of France, and in the larger cities. They were not to be found in the countryside, and most people had never heard of them. By 400 half the population may have been Christian; a rise from five to thirty million in less than a century. This was partly through conviction and partly through prudence. If the emperor became Christian this was enough to shock many into consideration of matters religious, and if a landowner became Christian the tenants on his estates would have to reconsider their position. But while the state might nudge it could not compel, for it was never as strong as a modern government. Of course Constantine had stripped many temples of their wealth to support his currency, and paganism with its need for a constant stream of animal sacrifices was more expensive than Christianity, but Constantine had scarcely touched pagans. It was not until the swing to Christianity had gained a degree of momentum that mobs and magistrates turned on the pagans. Until 380 Christians and pagans had got on fairly well, but after that date there were attacks on temples, and attacks on pagans. Some were tortured, and some died for their faith. From about 407 paganism could only live on in quiet corners of the empire.

Yet the final triumph would never have occurred without a major shift towards Christianity in the minds of men and women. And the shift was made more effective by paganism and Christianity sharing many things. A.D. Nock has written that 'Religious propaganda generally operates on the basis of a common cultural background or, as in modern missions, on superiority of culture.' Not all modern missions do operate on the basis of a superior culture, though Billy Graham benefits from the desirability of an American life-style. But the early church relied more on a common culture than on a superior one. And Christians and pagans did have much in common. They shared housing, work, cemeteries, and sometimes marriages. And increasingly they shared religious beliefs.

As Ramsay McMullen has put it, pagans became Christians with 'the least possible tear in the fabric of already held beliefs'. The ancient world was already turning to the idea of a single God, though it was not yet ready for the Christian insistence on turning other gods into mere demons. There is even evidence of pagan cults which went halfway towards Judaism. And the old pagan religion of interesting divinities of variable morality was gradually being replaced by a belief in the stars, or cosmic forces, or just blind fate. The gods were giving way to something grander, if something less friendly. Yet religion was only half the story. It was philosophy and not religion which, as Nock put it, 'offered intelligible explanations of phenomena'. Pagan religion was moving away from its roots and towards philosophy and yet, in the long run, pagan religion did not fit the philosophy of the day. It may have been because Christianity could and did that the Christians were able to ease out pagan religion while grabbing hold of pagan philosophy. This would mean that a convert would only have to deny half of the old heritage. And the half which was denied was the half which was least helpful in daily life.

If it is accepted that conversion works with a common cultural background, then the common background has to be really common. It is not just a matter of the future convert being near enough to Christianity for the final leap to be a small one. The Christians, or some of them, have to be near enough to paganism to remember what it meant to jump. They have to have one foot in the pagan world and one in the Christian. In a sense, they have to be bad Christians to be good evangelists. Fortunately for the church, there have always been a great many bad Christians. Billy Graham has not been one of them, and this may be why he is not really an evangelist, but a revivalist, reviving a faith which is the only one his hearers have ever known. So present-day courses

23

of instruction which attempt to make Christians better informed sometimes make them less effective evangelists

Yet Christianity made no startling demands on future converts. It called for something not far from what was already known and accepted. The idea of a god having a son was widespread in the ancient world. There were legends of a son of god dying, though not as a willing sacrifice. But what did jar on the ancient mind was the resurrection of the flesh. Getting away from it all meant getting away from the flesh, and a man was defined by Marcus Aurelius as 'a small soul carrying a dead body'. By rejecting the body Gnosticism was in many ways closer to the mainstream than was Christianity, and if much early preaching and teaching centred on this point it was for good reason. Yet even on this question popular belief may have been shifting. In the late Roman empire, even before the swing to Christianity, there was a shift from cremation to burial of the dead. This suggested the worth of the body, and its possibility for the future, instead of a mere desire to be rid of it.

But if Christianity spread slowly, how did the early Christians set about spreading their faith? The answer is that on the whole they did not. They kept a low profile. For over two centuries, until the emperor Constantine, there were no Christian missionaries and no Christian evangelists. There were writings about Christianity intended for outsiders, but there is not much evidence of these writings being read. Of course only one person out of four could read anyway, and when outsiders met Christianity it was more by face to face contact than anything else, and this is still very much the case in the modern world. But even if someone was attracted to the Christian faith, there was a good deal of reluctance to let that someone know too much about it. The apologists, those who wrote about Christianity, were almost without exception those who still had one foot in a non-Christian world. They were converts or the sons of converts.

The vast majority of Christians would seem to have been largely indifferent to the need to spread their faith. They knew that to argue with their neighbours could lead to violence; people do not enjoy being told that their gods are false. They knew that

they themselves were not popular, even if they seldom encoun-
tered actual persecution. They drew a line around themselves and
if others sought to cross that line, those others were usually family
friends or relatives or otherwise close to existing Christians. And
if Christians were drawn then, as they are today, mainly from the
'humble free classes', to quote Robin Lane Fox, they tended to
increase their ranks, however slowly, from those same classes.
There is no evidence that they ever sought to convert the millions
of slaves; only slaves of Christians would be brought into the
church.

In any event, it was unlikely that there would be anything like
mass evangelism in the early church. Mass evangelism depends
on there being a mass of people whose minds are all much the
same. This in its turn is linked to the idea that the Christian faith
is obvious to everyone, or at least to all unprejudiced people. In
modern times this has derived from Scottish 'common sense'
philosophy, but it is probably an outlook which can be found in
any age. Its effect is to place the emphasis on the preacher.
Attention is not given to those who are listening, since they
cannot differ from those who are already Christian, or differ
from one another. The people of the world are all one lump.

This brings us back to Billy Graham. There was a time when he
really was an evangelist, but that was when the church and the
world moved close to one another before moving past one
another and away. This happened in the early church for a while,
but it was not typical. For most of that period the Christians
were overwhelmingly similar to the Christians of Scotland in
1991, in that both lots inhabited rock-pools somewhat cut off
from society as a whole, and were glad to be cut off from society
as a whole. The tide might recede but they would stay as they
were; so much the worse for the tide. And the Billy Graham rally
would express a cultural distinctness which kept the world at a
distance.

Yet despite this lack of evangelism, there was a nearness to the
surrounding culture which meant that when particular sets of
ideas occurred, then outsiders could bridge the gaps. To complete
the seashore image, the tide would come in, and replenish the

rock-pool. But nobody then knew what would make the tide come in, and nobody knows now. All that we do know is that there are times which are suitable for mass evangelism, and times not suitable for mass evangelism. Which was stated long ago by that wise old bird, Billy Graham.

4

Irenaeus

'From the will and the wisdom of God, and from the virgin earth … God took dust of the earth and formed the man, the beginning of mankind. So then the Lord, summing up afresh this man, took the same dispensation of entry into flesh, being born from the Virgin by the will and wisdom of God, that he also should show forth the likeness of Adam's entry into the flesh …'

This is Irenaeus' doctrine of 'recapitulation' or going back over the whole thing again. It aimed at meeting the Gnostic doubts about the Old Testament by showing that the New Testament went over the events of the Old, but where the Old failed, the New did not. This served to anchor Christianity in history, against those who said it had no history. It also served to explain where the Old Testament fitted into the scheme of things. Of course Irenaeus did not invent this; it was used by Paul the Apostle in his well-known epistle to the Romans. But Irenaeus took it further. Not only did he make Christ a later or 'new' Adam, as Paul did, but he made the Virgin Mary a later and 'new' earth. Adam took flesh of the virgin earth, on which no rain had yet fallen, and Christ of the Virgin Mary.

'For it was necessary that Adam should be summed up in Christ, that mortality might be swallowed up and overwhelmed by immortality, and Eve summed up in Mary, that a virgin should be a virgin's intercessor, and by a virgin's obedience undo and put away the disobedience of a virgin.' Furthermore, 'the trespass which came by the tree was undone by the tree of disobedience', and the tree of knowledge in the garden of Eden replaced by the cross of Calvary. And if hymns tell us that 'A second Adam to the fight, and to the rescue came', they also tell of Christ dying upon the tree.

All of which is splendid stuff, but it has its drawbacks, whether it is done by Paul or done by Irenaeus. By the New Testament being made a re-run of the Old Testament, they are drawn too close together. It may be that the Gospels described the birth of Christ and the resurrection of Christ with contradictory details, possibly to show that what was being described was really undescribable. But in the long run it is clear that the Gospels mean the birth of Christ to be seen as a unique and real event, however it is expressed. And the same is true of the death of Christ and his resurrection. There are no successive Christs dying on successive crosses and rising again from successive tombs. There is something definite here, even if the descriptions do not agree on all points.

On the other hand, much of the Old Testament was a series of legends designed to convey, not an event, but a state of affairs. We get maximum understanding from reading of this state of affairs through different accounts. There are two accounts of creation; some would say three. There are a number of accounts of a fall from grace, and these are to be read in parellel, not as historical events happening one after another. The fall in the garden of Eden is one. The scattering of the human race after building the tower of Babel is another. There is the enmity between Cain and Abel. And Noah with his ark. And Noah's drunkenness. And the rebel angels of the Apocalypse (Revelation), which is really a bit of the Old Testament in the New. Each of these is enough in itself to affirm that there is something very wrong with the human race and, perhaps more important, that this is not how things were meant to be. This is not how they began.

But if we have a strong sense of Christ being the new Adam and the cross being the new tree, then the fall as described in the garden of Eden is not just one legend of many building up to a complete picture. It is the one and only account of the fall, and it governs everything else. Cain kills Abel because the snake tempted Eve who tempted Adam, and they build the tower of

Babel because they are already wicked thanks to the apple. These legends become historical events. The Old Testament becomes a history text-book. And quite apart from that, small details of the one and only legend of the fall become deeply significant. All females have their place in life determined by what is said to have happened in the garden. So do snakes, who also deserve better. But farmers do not have their place in life determined by Cain, or the engineering profession by the tower of Babel.

And if the Old Testament is interpreted in terms of the New, inevitably the New is going to be interpreted in terms of the Old. When it finally dawns on someone that most of Genesis is a collection of legends gathered together to set forth some truth, then the rest of the Old Testament and the New Testament are assumed to be legends in the same way. And, without going into the question of whether anything is what it says it is, or the other question of whether anything happened in history at all, there are parts of the Old Testament which are meant to be taken historically, and parts which are not, and the same is true of the New Testament. Irenaeus' theory makes it too easy. So does Paul's theory, but he does not take it as far as Irenaeus does.

As for the Irenaeus of history, he was Bishop of Lyons on the Rhone River in the south of France. That was a Greek colony, and Irenaeus himself came from Smyrna in Asia Minor. As he wrote of his childhood: 'I can tell the very place where the blessed Polycarp used to sit as he discoursed, his goings out and his comings in, the character of his life, his bodily appearance, the discourses he would address to the people, how he told of his conversation with John and with the others who had seen the Lord ...' He must have been born around the year 130, and lived until about 200. We know that he led a delegation from the church in Gaul to Rome, and after he became bishop rebuked Rome for excommunicating those who kept Easter on a weekday.

But his main writings were against the Gnostics and their claim that they had the true tradition from the apostles. Against this, Irenaeus pointed to the known succession of bishops, writing, 'we are in a position to number those who were made bishops in the churches by the apostles'. Furthermore, 'if the apostles had known hidden mysteries', they would have told these men, and not others who never set eyes on an apostle.

Irenaeus does not list all the churches since 'it would be very tedious', and whatever we may say of Irenaeus he is not that. Instead he refers to 'that tradition derived from the apostles, of the very great, the very ancient, and universally known church, founded and organized at Rome by the two most glorious apostles, Peter and Paul ... For it is necessary that every church, that is, the faithful everywhere, should get together with (some would translate it as 'agree with') this church, on account of its pre-eminent authority, in which the apostolical tradition has been preserved ...' He then lists its bishops from the start, and switches to Smyrna with another memory of Polycarp, and even refers to churches where they have no written scriptures, presumably because they cannot read, but keep the faith for all that.

Yet it is not just a succession of people, it is a succession of faith. And it is not just that either. Irenaeus looks back to show that there is continuing tradition, but he also teaches the 'living voice' of the church, inspired by the Spirit, which did not stop working in apostolic days. The living voice of tradition is not on paper, and it is not in words, but it is in people, for he is that sort of God. His delight is with people, and he works through people, and in saving his people he used human nature, and in keeping his church on the rails, he uses people again. He is a people sort of God. So the answer to whatever question comes up, and they are still coming up, is not to be found in some reference out there, like the metal bar in Paris which tells us how long is a metre, but by the whole Christian church thinking about it. Not by over-riding the human mind, but by using it, with the light given by the Spirit.

John Henry Newman distinguished between what he called 'Episcopal Tradition' and what he called 'Prophetical Tradition' in a series of sermons preached in 1836. Of the prophets he said, 'Their teaching is a vast system, not to be comprised in a few sentences, not to be embodied in one code or treatise, but consisting of a certain body of Truth, pervading the church like an atmosphere, irregular in its shape from its very profusion and exuberance; at times separable only in idea from Episcopal

Tradition, yet at times melting away into legend and fable; partly written, partly unwritten, partly the interpretation, partly the supplement of scripture, partly preserved in intellectual expressions, partly latent in the spirit and temper of Christians; poured to and fro in closets and on the housetops, in liturgies, in controversial works, in obscure fragments, in sermons, in popular prejudices, in local customs.' Which is what Irenaeus meant by the living voice. 'For where the church is,' wrote Irenaeus, 'there is the Spirit of God, and where the Spirit of God is, there is the church, and every kind of grace, but the Spirit is Truth.'

'But vain in every respect are they who despise the entire dispensation of God, and disallow the salvation of the flesh, and treat with contempt its regeneration ... But if this indeed do not attain salvation, then neither did the Lord redeem us with his blood, nor is the cup of the eucharist the communion of his blood, nor the bread which we break the communion of his body ...' So much for the Gnostic denial of the creation.

Finally, Irenaeus rested his case on his doctrine of God. Against the Gnostics, he made God creator, first, last, and always. 'He is the Former, he is the Builder, he is the Discoverer, he is the Creator, he the Lord of all ... He is Father, he is God, he the Founder, he the Maker, he the Creator, who made those things by himself.' The titles roll on and on, over and over, and so do the arguments. If God is supreme, how can he tolerate a world made by some lesser being? And a world made by angels against his will? And if God is so far from the world that the gap is unbridgeable, how can God be known? And do not the Gnostic emanations or radiations undermine the idea of an unbridgeable gap anyway?

And against the whole Gnostic scheme of angels, he set the 'two hands of God', of an active and involved God, in fact a loving God, the people sort of God, whose two hands are all he needs. 'It was not angels, therefore, who made us, nor who formed us ... For God did not stand in need of these ... as if he did not possess his own hands. For with him were always present the Word and the Wisdom, the Son and the Spirit, by whom, and in whom, freely and spontaneously, he made all things.'

31

God was active. God was direct. God was with people. That was Irenaeus.

5

Trinity

The simplest way to get some idea of the Trinity is to draw three dots in a triangle, all close together. Then repeat this with the dots further apart. The tight Trinity assumes that the humanity of Christ can be and is close to God the Father, while the loose Trinity assumes that there must be a great gulf between them. Otherwise humanity will be blasted by the holiness of the Father, and for humanity to come too close would be irreverent.

Behind this difference lie different views of humanity. If humanity is terribly sinful and God terribly holy, then there must be a large gap between them. If humanity is not all that sinful, then the gap need not be large at all. In theory there should be an ideal distance, but in practice the distance changes according to the cultural climate of the age. And it is only when it swings to one extreme or the other that it can be called a heresy, for heresy is not so much wrong thinking as right thinking taken to one extreme or the other. Where the Trinity was concerned, too tight a Trinity, in which the three dots really were one dot, was called Sabellianism, while too loose a pattern, in which the dots have no common factor, was called Arianism.

Sabellius was a Libyan who moved to Rome and headed one of the national or racial groups which made up the Roman church. Around the beginning of the third century he taught, or was said to have taught, that the Father and the Son and the Holy Spirit were identical. There were two ways of doing this, one saying that at his baptism Christ was adopted by the Father and received the person of the Father, and the other suggesting that God spent so many centuries as the Father, then ceased to be the Father and became the Son at Bethlehem, then ascended to heaven and returned as the Holy Spirit. This managed to avoid charges of worshipping more than one God, though that was about all it avoided. Sabellians were accused of crucifying the Father, and of turning God into a play-actor who pretended to be what he was not.

But most of what we know about Sabellius comes from a Roman presbyter named Hippolytus who had been overlooked in election to Bishop of Rome and did not take this in a kindly way. The successful candidate was one Callistus who, according to Hippolytus, had once been simultaneously slave and financial consultant, and whose investments went wrong, as they so often do. Callistus tried to escape by sea, leapt overboard, was rescued and put on the treadmill, was released then sent to the mines of Sardinia, was released again and became manager of the Christian cemetery, then aide to Zephyrinus the bishop, and finally his successor. If Hippolytus is to be believed (and he is probably not) Callistus tolerated Sabellius and copied his teaching, until Hippolytus made such a fuss that Callistus, 'a senseless and unstable fellow, who improvises blasphemies in every direction', finally condemned Sabellius and his creed. But this was not enough for Hippolytus who set himself up as rival bishop or 'antipope', only to be carted off to the mines of Sardinia in the next persecution from which he did not return alive. The story is helpful to counter the view that life in the early church was sweetness and light.

Sabellius' teaching came back to life in the person of Paul of Samosata, a Bishop of Antioch some sixty years later. Paul was reacting against speculations of Origen and insisted that Father and Son were as near the same as made no difference. A synod condemned him for his doctrine, not because 'he struts in the marketplace, reading and dictating letters as he walks in public', and not because in preaching 'he smites his hand with his thigh and stamps the tribunal with his feet, and those who do not applaud and wave their handkerchiefs, as in a theatre ... he rebukes and insults', and 'he trains women to sing psalms to

34

himself in the middle of the church on the great day of the Pascha, which would make one shudder to hear'. Well, we all know bishops like that.

If Sabellianism or Monarchianism or whatever we call it did not last long and did not involve a major split, it is at least a point of view which people still hold without realizing it. Fortunately it does not survive examination by the light of day, and it is reasonably harmless if the Sabellians in the south aisle of the church are balanced by Arians in the north aisle.

The story of Arius is not quite as simple. He was a presbyter in Alexandria, and if the pagan ideas of Rome led some Christians to exaggerate the unity of God, the Neo-Platonic 'oneness' thought of Egypt led some Christians to push the three persons of the Trinity too far apart. It all started when the bishop attempted 'too ambitious a discourse about the Holy Trinity', whereupon Arius, 'thinking that the bishop was introducing the doctrine of Sabellius the Libyan, from love of controversy advanced another view diametrically opposed ... If, he said, the Father begat the Son, he that was begotten has a beginning of existence, and from this it is evident, that there was when the Son was not.' In short, the Son must have been created, and was therefore not really God. The bishop was not sure what to do about all this and let everyone argue until 319, when he condemned Arius and his supporters. But that was only the beginning.

If Sabellius and his heresy were nothing too much, Arianism really took off. It spread and it spread and it touched a nerve on the body Christian. Somehow it filled a need for Christians to see God as holy and remote, and themselves as hopelessly depraved and utterly insignificant, so that the Father could not really have given his being to the Son who walked in Galilee. Or, for that matter, the Holy Spirit; could the Spirit dwelling in mere people really be the same as God? The Neo-Platonists who believed that God and people and everything else could be all wrapped up in a single smooth substance were probably a threat, and they may have pushed Christians in the opposite direction towards different substances. But it was a low view of themselves that made people Arian. And it still is.

But now the division over Arius was enough to worry the emperor, Constantine, who as a Christian did not want a divided church. He stepped in and started things moving. First, he sent a bishop from Spain, Hosius, to consult with the bishops of major cities. Secondly, he called a council of all bishops, or at least those in the East, to meet at what is now Ankara in Turkey. But he had to move carefully. As emperor he may have had a great deal of authority, but in the long run he could not use this authority in matters of faith without providing agreements which would then come unstuck. He could guide, he could influence, he could suggest, he could banish, but he could not decide. And already he had discovered that events were running away from him. Hosius had gone forth and consulted, but he had also excommunicated bishops who shared the views of Arius, including such moderates as Eusebius of Caesaria, who was later to become famous as the first church historian.

In 325 the council met at Nicaea, across the straits from Constantinople, and thus nearer to the emperor than Ankara. There were 220 bishops, all from the East, and two presbyters sent from Sylvester of Rome. Those who had been cast out by Hosius were allowed back, although Arius himself was condemned. A creed was accepted, though it was shorter than the so-called Nicene creed of today. Eusebius of Caesaria put forward one version, which he said was generally accepted, and 'our most pious emperor, before anyone else, testified that it was most orthodox', but wanted the addition of a word, '*homoousios*', meaning that Father and Son were of the 'same substance'. Of course Constantine did not think this up on his own; it had been around for some time and he hoped it would end the argument, which it did not. And the bishops then went on to regulate the time of preparation for baptism, the morals of the clergy, the penitents of one church trying to get pardoned in another, the holding of local synods, the consecrations of new bishops by all bishops in that province, or at least by three of them, and the recognition of the sacraments of heretics brought back into the church. There was a good deal about keeping deacons in their places, which were lowly places, and some rules about deaconesses which are puzzling indeed. And the bishops went home.

Where things looked rather different, away from the emperor and his officials and the pressures of Nicaea. And some began to have second thoughts. The word *homoousios* was not in the New Testament, and there was room for confusion as to whether it meant 'the same substance' or 'the same bit of substance', and quite sensible people wondered if they had not gone too far. A less sensible man called Eusebius of Nicomedia (not the church historian) admitted Arius to communion, was sent into exile, came back, and persecuted his opponents. Athanasius, Bishop of Alexandria after the famous Alexander who started it all off with his too ambitious sermon, was such an opponent of Arius that he was sent to exile in France. However, this was partly for being rough with schismatics in Egypt, and partly for threatening a dock strike which would have deprived Constantinople of wheat. On top of this a bishop in Ankara argued that I Cor. 15.28, 'then the Son himself will also be made subordinate to God', was against the Nicaean formula, and was duly exiled in turn. Meanwhile Arius died, and Constantine died, and there was more confusion as bishops in the West tried to sort out the question, and failed.

In 346 there was an imperial compromise. Athanasius was allowed back into Egypt, while the bishop from Ankara was thrown to the wolves, who perhaps deserved to have him. Then Constantius consolidated his power and moved against the Nicaean group; Athanasius fled to the desert for his second exile. Bishops were replaced by those who taught that Father and Son were not of the same substance, nor even of like substance, but of unlike substance, and 'the world groaned to find itself Arian'. In fact the groaning did not last. The problem was beginning to sort itself out.

If the hero of all this was Athanasius, this was partly because his writings inspired so many of his day, and after. He has been described as 'Athanasius contra mundum', or Athanasius against the world, and has ever been an inspiration to all sorts of blockheads who think that because they are all alone in their views they must be like Athanasius. But the truth is that Athanasius was never alone; despite appearances his position was really that of the centre of the church. Again, he was no fanatic, and went out of his way to recognize the intentions if not the exact wordings of some of his more moderate opponents. He is known for many things, not least the doctrine that 'God became man, that man might become God'. It is a dangerous doctrine, and in unskilled hands it can mean that we cease to be individuals and are all dissolved into one divine substance like peanut butter, but there is a sense in which it is true.

The others who tidied up the doctrine of the Trinity were the Cappadocian fathers, Basil of Caesarea, Gregory of Nyssa, and Gregory of Nazianzus. Around 375 Basil defined the Trinity as falling between two falsehoods when he wrote that 'as he who fails to confess the community of the essence falls into polytheism, so he who refuses to grant the distinction of the persons is carried away into Judaism.' And in a later work he dealt with knowing God. 'What is the essence of the object of worship? If I confess that I am ignorant of the essence, they turn on me and say, So you worship you know not what.' And he continued, 'The operations are various, and the essence simple, but we say that we know our God from his operations, but do not undertake to approach near to his essence. His operations come down to us; but his essence remains beyond our reach.'

Yet the last word belongs to Gregory of Nazianzus. 'My inclination is to avoid all assemblies of bishops, because I have never seen any council come to a good end, nor turn out to be a solution of evils. On the contrary it usually increases them.' We all feel that way about church gatherings, and usually with some justice, but there is no other way. Councils and synods and conventions and assemblies are a terrible price to pay for the joys of the Christian life, but it is a price which must be paid.

6

Persecution

In the summer of 1940 when Britain stood alone or almost alone before Hitler, a church paper called *The Record* expressed some hesitation about troops from Europe, presumably Poles and Czechs and French. According to *The Record*, 'it is left to us now to fight and pay for the war in our own way, and if they are only asked to give up Sunday soccer they are indeed fortunate'. This Sunday soccer was 'definitely not in the national interest', 'when we are expecting so much from God'.

The idea that God would favour Hitler rather than a nation whose allies played soccer on Sunday may seem a trifle bizarre. But in times of stress it is natural to blame those who have not pulled their weight in the common interest and have thus offended whatever gods there be. So with the early Christians. They may not have done anything which was actually criminal, but when the gods looked down to see that everyone was offering sacrifice, they would note that some were not, and would react accordingly. The only way to be safe was to make the Christians offer sacrifice like decent citizens or,if that failed, to have a go at whatever Christians were to be found in some dark alley.

It is a favourite theme of preachers that persecution is a good thing. The blood of the martyrs becomes the seed of the church. This idea of martyrdom was popular around the time of the First World War, when poets such as Patrick Pearse believed that 'bloodshed is a cleansing and sanctifying thing'. The result was a devotion to 'lesser Calvaries', to quote a hymn often sung on 11 November, and the assumption that Christ's sacrifice on the cross

39

was not enough. As Pearse wrote of trench warfare: 'Such august homage was never being offered to God as this, the homage of millions of lives given gladly for love of country.' Nor was this just a fancy of poets; in one of the *Anne of Green Gables* books a minister in Prince Edward Island pronounces in 1914, 'Our race has marked every step of its painful ascent with blood. And now torrents of it must flow again ... it is the price humanity must pay for some blessing – some advance great enough to be worth the price ...' We may wonder if a fictional minister is more real than a non-fictional poet, but the real question is whether this idea came from a distorted view of early Christian martyrs, or whether the view of the martyrs was distorted by the desperate attempt to make sense of carnage in the trenches.

History does not support the idea that persecution led to growth, and neither does common sense. Mild and temporary disapproval or even violence may make Christians think, but serious persecution leads to division, suspicion, and eventually to there being no Christians at all. If the persecution is as concentrated as that of the Turks against the Armenians in 1916, then it will clear the country, and there is nothing that can be done about it. Fortunately, states rarely can concentrate enough resources to wipe out Christianity. But they can and do disrupt it, and they cause immense suffering. And the idea that God intended his followers, whom he claimed to love, to be tortured so that his kingdom might be extended, or that his will could only be achieved by mutilation and murder, is grotesque. It argues that God was making converts by lying to them about what the Christian life really was. It is one thing to say that Christians may be persecuted, but another to say that this is a good thing. As for those who quote the saying of Tertullian, that the blood of the martyrs was the seed of the church, they would do well to consider that in the physiology of the ancient world it was believed that human seed was a refined form of blood, and that if this is no longer believed the saying does not make sense.

At first persecution was a question of popular dislike and mob violence, with the crowds insisting that officials put Christians to death, while the officials who did not like public outbursts wanted to keep the peace. As for emperors, they were more protective than vindictive, though an occasional tyrant such as Nero would gladly blame the Christians for the burning of Rome and distract attention by having them publicly put to death, 'not so much for the crime of arson as for hatred of the human race'. But with the passing of nearly two centuries, from the horrors of Nero in 64 until the formal persecution by the Emperor Decius in 250, the average inhabitant had come to know that Christians were a bit odd and did not eat with pagans, but also that Christians were otherwise a fairly ordinary lot who could hardly be guilty of terrible crimes. In the cities of the Roman empire there was very little privacy, and if some Christians could arrange to share living space, others could not. Everyone knew who the Christians were, and everyone knew what they were like. The mobs could not be roused against Christians, and the danger now came from the emperors. If only a couple of hundred Christians were to die for their faith in the first two centuries, thousands were to follow once persecution became formal.

But even they only really persecuted Christians as an accidental by-product of higher aims, just as they persecuted other religions and cults which offended them from time to time. It is nice to be able to think about the early Christians struggling in a life and death battle against evil emperors determined to exterminate them, but in fact the emperors were not usually determined to do any such thing. Decius was aware that his right to the throne was pretty shaky, and he decided that to make himself look better he would require everyone to sacrifice to the old Roman gods. It was just bad luck that there happened to be some people in the empire who had some sort of scruple about this.

But it turned out that many Christians had no scruples about this, and it seems likely that most Christians quite cheerfully burned incense to the genius of the emperor, rather like paying a tax – something which might go against the grain, but hardly important. There was a massive rejection of Christianity, but there were also Christians who burned incense to the gods on Tuesday and then rolled up for church on Sunday without thinking anything of it. It was to take time before the church

41

could bring back teaching on the need to witness to Christ. The relatively few martyrs were to have their stories told again and again to stiffen the resolve of the others.

The tales of the martyrs were many and varied; so were the martyrs. Ignatius of Antioch, bishop and Roman citizen, was taken to Rome to be put to death around about 110, visiting the churches of Asia Minor on the way, and writing epistles in which his coming sacrifice gave him some added authority as he urged them to respect their bishops and reject false teachings. But he also steeled himself for the ordeal ahead. 'Let there come on me fire and cross and conflicts with wild beasts, wrenching of bones, mangling of limbs, crushing of the whole body, grievous torments of the devil may I but attain to Jesus Christ.' Polycarp, the aged Bishop of Smyrna on the Aegean coast, who had known the apostle John, was put to death around 155. At first he withdrew to the country; this was sometimes done to avoid stirring up the mob. But two of his young slaves were tortured, a common feature of these stories, and Polycarp was found and taken to the stadium where he refused to deny Christ, saying, 'Eighty-six years have I served him, and he has done me no wrong ; how then can I blaspheme my King who saved me?' The officials did their best to avoid burning someone of such high social rank, but he remained faithful to Christ, and the fire was lit. The account has it that 'The fire made the appearance of a vaulted roof ... in the midst, not like flesh burning, but like a loaf baking, or like gold and silver being refined in a furnace. Moreover we caught a fragrance as of the breath of frankincense or some other precious spice.' The images of gold and frankincense are obvious; the offertory of bread in the eucharist likewise, and what must have been a horrible sight was presented as a triumph.

So also with Blandina, one of the martyrs at Lyons in 177, of whom we are told that 'those who by turns kept torturing her in every way from dawn till evening were worn out and exhausted', and Perpetua and Felicitas at Carthage in 203 where Perpetua was described as becoming male in her martyrdom – either a relic of Gnostic thought or an application of Aristotle's belief that females were potential males who had failed to be properly formed in the womb. But when Decius' persecution broke out in 250, Cyprian the Bishop of Carthage, who was himself to be blamed for retreating to a safe place, though later he died bravely, wrote of the general response of the Christians. 'They did not even wait to be arrested before they went up, or questioned before they made their denial.' 'How many the magistrates put off at the time, as night was at hand!'

If the persecution of Decius was an administrative nightmare, that of Valerian from 257 was more selective. The clergy would be taken, and the sacred books would be destroyed, and the rank and file could be left to find their own way back to Roman worship. But, as so often, the state had more important things to do, and emperors were short-lived, and the persecution passed. It was Diocletian who unleashed the last wave of persecution in 303, concentrating first on buildings and books, and then on clergy, and in the following year requiring sacrifice by all. But this was in fact a very limited effort, scarcely noted in the Western parts of the empire, and sporadic even in the East. Yet we have stories which are gripping enough. 'When it was yet hardly light, the prefect, together with chief commanders, tribunes and officers of the treasury, came to the church in Nicomedia; they forced the doors and searched everywhere for an image of the god. The Holy Scriptures were found and burnt; the church was abandoned to general pillage ... Then Praetorian Guards came in battle array, with axes and other tools; they were let loose everywhere, and in a few hours, levelled that very lofty edifice with the ground. Next day an edict was published, depriving the Christians of all honours and dignities ... they should be subject to torture ...' Of course there was no image of the god; it was not that sort of god.

At Cirta in North Africa, the local official told Paul, the bishop, to 'bring out the writings of the law ... ', and the bishop rather evasively said that the readers had the scriptures, but handed over what he had. He was then commanded to name the readers, but said, 'The municipal office knows them, that is, the clerks Edusius and Junius,' thereby avoiding the sin of naming them himself. After this, they took the church plate and large stores of clothing and footwear, in the presence of three priests, two deacons, four sub-deacons, and some 'diggers'. Asked to name the readers, two sub-deacons replied, 'We are not traitors; here we are, order us to be killed,' but eventually named one reader, and the clerks of the municipal office named the rest. Four handed over their books, one said he had none, one was out but his wife handed over his books. The impression given is of officials who know all about the Christians, and are only doing what they have to do, and Christians who are not sure how far they can go without being traitors on the one hand or being put to death on the other.

For it was seldom black and white but, like most moral decisions, shades of grey. If someone who handed over books was a 'traditor' (traitor), what of somebody who pointed out the man who had the books? Was it a mortal sin to hand over clothing and footwear? Was it a mortal sin to hand over medical texts to illiterate slaves who thought they were scripture? And was it a sin to move away? Polycarp fled and his servants were tortured. Cyprian fled and other bishops were martyred. But some bishops may have caused persecution by not getting out of the way when tempers were inflamed. And then there is the reader whose wife handed over his books; to what extent was he to blame? And in most cases punishment fell upon whole families; should Christians cause their wives and children to suffer if those wives and children were not so inclined? And what was the position of a Christian wife whose pagan husband sacrificed for her, or a Christian wife whose Christian husband sacrificed for her?

These questions arose when persecution had passed and churches had to decide what to do with those who had denied Christ. On the one hand, those who had stood firm and refused to sacrifice were not likely to welcome back the masses who had first sacrificed and then, when it was safe to do so, regretted it. Those whose nearest relatives had been put to death could hardly be blamed for their martyrdom being regarded as worthless. But the vast bulk of Christians could hardly be cast aside, unless it was desired that the church should be small and pure – and completely dwarfed by another church of those who had failed in the hour of trial but might, in the future, be more constant, and who were trying to be Christian in a muddled way. The result almost everywhere was division. There were those who claimed that once a Christian had denied Christ the decision was binding, and there was no way back. 'Once to every man and nation, comes the moment to decide,' and that moment would never return. But there were also those, usually a majority, who were willing to allow Christians who had sacrificed and then repented to attend church at the back, sometimes in pentitential clothing, for months or years until they might be re-admitted to holy communion.

The situation was especially critical in the North African centre of Carthage where the bishop, Cyprian, had gone underground. This did not impress the rigorists who observed that other bishops in the area had been put to death. At first Cyprian offered no mercy to the lapsed, but after peace came in 251 he did agree to accept them back and to absolve them from their sin of denial. And, so that there might not be centres of easier reconciliation, primitive tax-havens, he advised Rome of his decision. Yet Cyprian was then faced with a schism in Carthage, and wrote on the unity of the church: 'The episcopate is one; it is a whole in which each bishop enjoys full possession. The church is likewise one, though she is spread abroad, and multiplies with the increase of her progeny: even as the sun has rays many, yet one light; and the tree, boughs many, yet its strength is one, seated in the deep-lodged root ...' Again; 'he who leaves the church of Christ, attains not to Christ's rewards. He is an alien, an outcast, an enemy. He can no longer have God for a father who has not the church for a mother. If any man was able to escape who was outside the ark of Noah, then will that man escape who is out of doors beyond the church.'

Meanwhile in Rome the bishop was dead, and there were two candidates, Cornelius who favoured pardoning the lapsed, and Novatian who did not. Cornelius was elected but Novatian, as Cornelius put it in words which may not be entirely impartial, 'chose to himself two companions who had renounced their own salvation, that he might send them to a small and very insignificant part of Italy, and entice thence by some made-up devices three bishops, rough and very simple men'. They having arrived in Rome 'were shut up by certain disorderly men like himself, and at the tenth hour, when they were drunk, and sick with the after effects, he forcibly compelled them to give him a bishop's office by a counterfeit and vain laying on of hands ...' The Novationist schism spread throughout the empire, but as it was a schism relating to the past its influence was doomed to fade, and its followers eventually found their way back into the mainstream.

That, of course, created new problems. The church which allowed penance and absolution for those who had denied Christ could hardly refuse to allow penance and absolution for those who had denied the church, but should ordination in a schismatic church be recognized, and should baptism in a schismatic church be recognized? Cyprian demanded that converts should be re-baptized, 'because the church is one, and baptism cannot be out of the church', though Stephen of Rome took the opposite view. Cyprian wrote that 'among other things arrogant or extraneous or self-contradictory, which he wrote without due instruction and caution' Stephen had written that former heretics and schismatics should have hands laid on for forgiveness, and nothing more. The argument then switched to the authority of Stephen as successor to Peter, which Cyprian acknowledged, though he also insisted that 'every bishop in the free use of his liberty and power has the right of forming his own judgment, and can no more be judged by another than he can himself judge another'. Stephen died in 256 and two years later Cyprian was put to death in Valerian's persecution. Their difference was not overcome in their lifetime, and is not yet overcome; the East rejects all sacraments in schismatic churches while the West does not.

But one schism lingered on. About 311 the Bishop of Carthage died and a group of coastal bishops hastily elected Caecilian whose main consecrator was Felix, of whom it was said, rightly or wrongly, that he had given up books to the persecutors. When seventy inland Numidian bishops arrived to find they were too late, they said the consecration was invalid because of Felix, and they were supported by a rich widow who had been forbidden to kiss the knuckle-bone of a martyr before receiving holy communion. The split may have been influenced by race and class, but the excuse was martyrdom. And in a time and place where many if not most Christians were cut off from communion for sexual reasons, martyrs were vital as their merits were seen to be available to the less heroic. But whatever the ultimate cause, a rival bishop was consecrated, and his successor was Donatus, whose name was given to the movement. It thrived on memories of the martyrs, and when it was persecuted by the majority party, with state support, it had new martyrs. Indeed, martyrdom was a theme in pre-Christian religion of that area. After the Islamic invasion the Donatists were wiped out or died out; in mediaeval times Islamic persecution destroyed the majority church as well. But the reverence to martyrs lingered on in North African Islam; there is a famous tale of a traveller beset by bandits who sought to save his life by pleading that he was of the blood of the Prophet, whereupon his delighted captors took him to their village where they slew him so that they could build him a shrine.

After Diocletian left office in 305, there was virtual toleration until the Edict of Milan in 313 made it official. But that was not quite the watershed which we sometimes assume. For most Christians before that date there was no persecution in their lifetime, or if there was persecution it was in a distant part of the empire. Persecution was limited in time and in locality. After that date, the church was to be favoured in the Roman empire, but persecuted beyond that empire, and in the succeeding centuries there were to be periods of sporadic persecution. This is much as might be expected. The aims of the church and of the state, any state, may overlap, but they can never be the same. Since most states and virtually all churches favour the well-being of the people, there is room for co-operation, but there is also misunderstanding when a church is assumed to be the willing servant of a state. And there can be more than misunderstanding; the age of the martyrs, numerically, is not the age of the early church but of this century. Christians cannot expect to be comfortable. And they probably won't be, even if they expect to be.

7

Christ

In Islamic theology, Muhammed is the Prophet to whom the Koran was given; it was written in heaven and dictated to him. In Christian theology, the Bible comes through Christ and it was Christ who came down from heaven. Thus it is not surprising that Muslims have spent much time arguing over the nature of the Koran and little over the nature of Muhammed, while the early Christians devoted much time to the person of Christ, and quite a bit less to the Bible.

If there were two ways of looking at the Trinity, depending on whether humanity was considered good or bad, the same was true of christology, the doctrine of the person of Christ. A poor view of humanity led to Arianism – the very loose Trinity in which Christ is so far from the Father as to be not even divine. A high view of humanity led to such a tight Trinity that Father, Son, and Holy Spirit were all one person, which is called Sabellianism. On the subject of the Person of Christ, a low view of humanity can go so far as to say that there is no humanity at all in Christ. This is Monophysitism – the doctrine of one nature, and a divine nature, in Christ. The opposite extreme has it that there is so much humanity in the person of Christ that the human is actually a separate person. Instead of one person, there are two. This is called Nestorianism, and historically there are links between Sabellians and Nestorians. If there are no historical links between Arians and Monophysitites, there should be, but nothing in this world is perfect.

We begin with Nestorius, one of those holy monks from

Antioch who had been made Bishop of Constantinople on the grounds that most bishops were too worldly and a simple monk would be better. He was not. Nestorius was a follower of Theodore of Mopsuestia, a man orthodox enough but inclined to push the two natures of Christ a little too far apart. For this reason he opposed the title *Theotokos* for the Virgin Mary. *Theotokos* meant God-bearer, and strictly speaking it should have been Christ-bearer, but the title had been used for so long in such an orthodox way that Nestorius' tactless attack led to the idea that he did not think the humanity of Christ was joined to the divinity. In 428 Nestorius was attacked by Cyril of Alexandria, and only the favour of the emperor saved him. Cyril then said the two natures were joined in one being (*hypostasis*) which is virtually the same as person, so you could say God was born of Mary. 'If anyone in the one Christ divides the personalities, that is the human and divine, after the union, connecting them only by a connection of dignity or authority or rule, and not rather by a union of natures, let him be condemned.' The Emperor Theodosius wavered according to whether he was under the spell of his wife or his sister. The Romans got involved in the belief that it had something to do with Pelagianism, which was the only heresy they really understood and which they tended to read into everything. Then Theodosius called a council at Ephesus for 431.

It lacked a certain something. To begin with, Cyril and the other Egyptians excommunicated Nestorius. As Nestorius wrote many years later, 'I was summoned by Cyril, who assembled the council, by Cyril, who presided. Who was judge? Cyril. Who was accuser? Cyril. Who was Bishop of Rome? Cyril. Cyril was everything.' In fact Cyril had hurried matters along before the arrival of the Syrian bishops who were travelling overland. When the Syrians arrived, they excommunicated Cyril and, for good measure, the Bishop of Antioch. Representatives from Rome arrived and supported Cyril, in exchange for which he condemned the Pelagian heresy. The emperor ordered all excommunicated bishops imprisoned, which usually speeds up decisions.

But despite all this, some theological truths did emerge.

Nestorius had gone too far and was losing support. He had denied the hypostatic union (in one person) of the two natures, and said that the two natures were only united in one will. This was close to a form of Sabellianism in which the divinity reaches out to collaborate with the man Jesus. Nestorius was sent back to his monastery and in 436 exiled to Upper Egypt where he wrote a book which, in the rather chaotic publishing world of the day, got lost until 1897. It showed that he was a more orthodox person than had been believed.

So much for Nestorius, but in the eastern reaches of the Roman empire his doctrine lived on for many years, and he is still regarded as a saint amongst the so-called Assyrian Christians who have, with the Kurds, suffered in the mountains of Iraq after the Gulf War of 1991. Under Ibas of Edessa the Nestorian version of Christianity was taught in the Persian empire. But the most notable relic of Nestorian Christianity is the famous 'Nestorian Monument', an inscribed stone covered with fine writing in both Chinese and Syriac, set up in China in 781 and telling the tale of the arrival of missionaries, notably one Alopen, from Persia in 635. The writing continued the story of that lost church of China, and gave an unusual but orthodox description of the Christian faith. The church perished under persecution, and the stone was buried under rubble, only to be dug up accidentally in 1625 and to be used by Jesuit missionaries to show that Christianity was really not alien to Chinese history.

But if Nestorius was not as much of a heretic as people thought, the great Cyril of Alexandria was more. That he is now a saint of the church is by selective reading in his works; his attacks on Nestorius never made many friends, and he disliked using the word *hypostasis* for person, preferring *phusis* which could mean nature. This meant that he could be supposed to say that in Christ there was only one nature, a divine nature, so that Christ was not human at all. And that is the Monophysite or one-nature heresy, which many modern Christians find congenial though they have never heard the name. It rules out humanity altogether, and this is attractive to those whose view of human nature is so dark that they think it needs to be ruled out. But it means that any sacrifice offered by Christ is not done on behalf of the human race, since Christ is not of that race.

Yet Cyril's triumph was short-lived. His Latin friends were too far away to be helpful, and in the long run he had to accept a compromise with John of Antioch. The 433 Formulary to which he agreed said that Christ was 'of one substance with the Father in his godhead, of one substance with us in his manhood, so that there is a union of two natures; on which ground we confess Christ to be one and Mary to be the Mother of God'. Despite the last phrase on *theotokos*, this leaned a little more to the Antioch side of the argument, and Cyril's followers were never very happy about it. When he died an opponent wrote sourly, 'Those who live on after him are delighted to lose him, but perhaps the dead are not so happy. People here are troubled in case the dead are so upset at having Cyril amongst them that they will send him back to us …'

It was after Cyril's death that the Alexandrines tried to get a better deal. The more radical Monophysites were now gathered around a monk called Eutyches, whose godfather was an influential eunuch in the emperor's court. These two joined the new Bishop of Alexandria, Dioscoros, in a plan to overthrow the compromises of 431 and 433. Eutyches attacked these, and was deposed by Flavian, Bishop of Constantinople, but appealed for aid to the Romans. The emperor, moved by the eunuch, then called another council at Ephesus to meet in 449 – and to be known in history as the robber-council or 'latrocinium'.

But things had changed in Rome, which normally supported Alexandria through reliance on Egyptian grain and fear of Sabellianism. Leo was now bishop, and he was one Westerner who understood more than six-guns. He saw that Eutyches argued for 'one nature after the union' which meant a form of Monophysitism in which the person of Christ mixed divinity and humanity into one smooth substance which was neither one thing nor the other. It could not redeem us as it was not human, and could not have the power to do so as it was not divine. Of course Leo would not attend a council, as he regarded councils as Eastern and local, which the West would accept or reject when they were all over. But he sent representatives and a 'Tome' or statement, which Dioscorus refused to have read. The proceedings were thoroughly partisan. Flavian was deposed and imprisoned and so badly beaten that he died, while a great many other bishops, whether truly Nestorian or not, were deposed and replaced by men of Alexandrine outlook. But this was such a one-sided council that it was certain not to be the last word, and it wasn't. The Emperor Theodosius fell off his horse and died. The power behind the robber-council died with him.

It was the emperor's sister who stepped into the gap, married a soldier who became emperor, put the eunuch to death for crimes both ecclesiastical and civil, and exiled Eutyches. In 451 there was a new council at Chalcedon across the straits from Constantinople. Dioscoros was deposed. Nestorius was still condemned, but his supporters were restored to their bishoprics. Leo's agents were still waving his 'Tome' and trying to read it in Latin, while the Eastern bishops shouted, 'Peter has spoken through Leo' (or maybe they didn't). That there was one person and two natures became Chalcedonian orthodoxy: 'He is God, of the Substance of the Father, begotten before the worlds : and he is Man, of the Substance of his Mother, born in the world. Perfect God : perfect Man, of reasoning soul and human flesh subsisting. Equal to the Father as touching his Godhead : less than the Father as touching his Manhood. Who although he be God and Man : yet he is not two, but one Christ.' So thundered the so-called Athanasian creed, 'which except a man do faithfully and stedfastly believe, he cannot be saved'.

Which was all very well, but some did not. They were still worried about the two natures, which they took to be two people, and when a Chalcedonian bishop in Alexandria was murdered his successor was a Monophysite, a believer in one-nature. And there was nothing anyone could do to stop it; the Egyptian church and the Ethiopian church were Monophysite and remained so. In Constantinople itself chariot-racing teams wore either blue, which meant Chalcedonian, or green, which meant tending to Monophysitism. (There is an echo of this in modern Athens where football teams are either politically conservative in outlook, with the double-headed eagle of the Byzantine emperors as their badge, or radical with, mysteriously, an Irish shamrock.)

Of course there were attempts to find a common way. The Emperor Zeno in 482 propounded a lovely document which really said nothing at all, and this was accepted in Alexandria and Antioch but not in Rome, and then the Emperor Justinian made a great show of being Chalcedonian while permitting his wife to make a great show of not being Chalcedonian, so that everybody felt that their side was really going to come out on top. But outright schism could only be delayed; in due course a wandering bishop named Jacob set up an underground church of the stricter Monophysites in Syria, and the Jacobites (not to be confused with Scottish supporters of the House of Stuart who were given the same name) have been a feature of Christian life from that day to this. Armenia was added to the Monophysite camp, though without really holding the doctrines, and in due course so were some in India.

Then came Monothelitism, a doctrine that there were two natures but only one will, which appeared in the seventh century and was accepted by Rome in a weak moment. It was shown to be only a new version of Monophysitism by Maximus the Confessor – a very attractive figure – and it only survived in the Lebanon, where its adherents lived in the mountains. Centuries later they linked themselves to Crusaders, and thus to Rome, and are now the Maronite Christians of that land. They deny having ever been heretics, and perhaps they are right.

But the last phase of this argument, in so far as there can be a last phase to any argument, was in iconoclasm, a word meaning 'breaking of images'. In the West this was taken to be a puritan reaction against idolatry, but the question ran deeper than that. It was whether the humanity of Christ was so real that his picture could be painted. It was one of the remarkable things about early Christianity that nobody knew or apparently wanted to know what Christ looked like. And not only that, some did not want pictures of the saints either, since they were in glory and thus, it was assumed, no longer bodily in form.

Nonetheless, pictures and statues of Christ and the saints did become common and in the year 726 soldiers tore down an image of Christ over the gate of the imperial palace at Constantinople. When onlookers protested some were killed. In this period a similar wave of image-breaking passed over Islam, and a common belief in the remoteness of God seems to have surfaced in different forms. In Constantinople there were more riots, a patriarch was deposed, Rome protested, and the monks emerged as champions of icons while the army opposed them. In 754 the Council of Hieria forbade all forms of icons, and said that Christ could only be seen in this world under the forms of bread and wine. But the death of the emperor led his widow, Irene, to call the Second Council of Nicaea in 787.

This council supported icons, and set up elaborate rules for their display. Eventually only flat images were permitted, with double haloes around the face of Christ, and single haloes around the faces of saints, to indicate that they were in glory. Icons became so important to the East that the iconostasis, or icon-stand before the altar, turned into a wall blocking off the normal view of that altar, and then the icons were regarded with such reverence that sometimes metal covers were placed over all the icon except the face and hand. It is ironic, if not iconic, that the battle to ensure the full humanity of Christ and thus human access to Christ, should have led to access to the eucharistic mystery being blocked by those same icons which were to have guaranteed this.

But behind all these complicated negotiations and disagreements there is a basic question. How corrupt are we? Is our life really one of money-making and self-indulgence? Are cruelty and indifference to the sufferings of others the natural way in which to be human? If this is so, then it means that societies must govern by stick and by carrot, and there can be no appeal to a good side of human nature which does not exist. Only the market can bring results. With a very strong police and a constant threat of being dumped in the street.

And, of course, if this is true then it means that that sort of nature cannot be in Jesus Christ. He could not be human. His 'one nature' had to be divine, and nothing else. On the other hand, if

54

there is really something worthwhile in humanity, then there can be two natures – and if humanity is very good indeed, there can be two persons or something very near to two persons. But the evidence of our daily life suggests that Nestorianism will always be a minority option.

8

Worship

While the councils of the church deliberate and the emperors persecute or otherwise, and while great things are done in great places, the worship of the church continues. Often without anyone bothering to describe what is done, since everyone knows about it anyway. With the result that we are not well informed on the matter today. Our descendents, if the nuclear threat allows us to have any, may want to know how many swipes of the sponge an average twentieth-century dweller needs in order to take a bath, but there is no information about it in any encyclopaedia. Everybody knows how to take a bath, except the masses of people who do not have baths, and who are usually forgotten. In the early church, everybody knew how to worship, and they only bothered to write about it if they went somewhere else and found something different. Fortunately, they sometimes did go somewhere else, or they had things they only did rarely and therefore had to do by numbers, so we do have some information.

First, they had a calendar. In those days every religion had a calendar, and to begin with the Christians had the Jewish calendar of weeks with certain yearly festivals. Easter was something of a problem, since it could either be kept on a Sunday, in the seven-day cycle, or on the 14th day of Nisan, in the 365-day cycle. Since the Christians kept Sunday as the Day of Resurrection it did not make sense to keep the annual festival of Resurrection on some other day, so the 14th of Nisan was abandoned and the link with the Jewish Passover was weakened. For a while the

Jewish Sabbath was kept beside the Christian Sunday, and in some places actually kept in the synagogue, but this could not and did not last. Pentecost was a Jewish as well as a Christian festival, and Ascension Day came later.

Christmas was a latecomer, widely adopted in the fourth century. It was placed at the point in the year where the days are shortest, to use that critical point which would otherwise be used by others, and to ease the conversion of sun-worshippers. Images of the winter sun, a round red Santa Claus, a round red robin, a round red holly-berry, and a round red mail-coach travelling right to left, are still popular on Christmas cards. And this neatly demonstrated the words of John in the Gospel, 'He must increase and I must decrease,' for in the half-year from the birth-date of John the Baptist, June 24, the sun decreases, and in the half-year from the birth-date of Christ it increases. But the mid-winter calendar has December 25 and January 1 and January 6, the last now related to Wisemen from the East but originally an alternative Christmas. They were all supposed to mark the shortest day of the year but got a bit lost.

And then there were festivals of the dead, usually fixed at the start of November when vegetation was dying but one vegetable was flourishing – the pumpkin. Since this is more or less round and can hold a candle, it is also an image of the declining sun, yellow and not yet red. And because it is an image of the sun, it can also be an image of Christ. It is no accident that when Cinderella, who represents the ashes of the dead, goes to meet the Prince, she does so in a pumpkin. She leaves a slipper to commit herself, just as children hang up stockings and not T-shirts on Christmas eve, and just as Marie in *The Nutcracker* supported the Nutcracker against the Mouse King by throwing her slipper into the battle.

But the calendar which resulted is a mixture. There are the seven-day cycles of weeks, which were Jewish. There is a twelve-month cycle based on the moon, which was Roman. There are festivals based on the moon but occurring once a year, and festivals related to the sun but also once a year, and conflicting with those based on the moon. But this is normal; the secular world uses a seven-day week which has nothing to do with a 365 day year, and even that year starts on January 1 for most purposes, but on April 6 for tax purposes, the former being Scots and the latter English, which may tell us something of those two peoples, though it would be imprudent to suggest what.

Baptism was naturally modelled on washing, and if there was a great deal of anointing this was then part of the process of taking a bath. The best way to understand early baptism is to go to a shop selling bath salts and bubbles and lotions. Since there was no soap, it was customary to rub the body with oil, or have this done by a bath attendant, and then wash the dirt off together with the oil. There would then be more oil, which was perfumed and offset body odours. But that was not all. There would first be a rejection of sin, then the washing, and then the laying on of hands by the bishop with further anointing. This last was for the gift of the Holy Spirit, and it was long argued whether the critical part was the laying on of hands or the anointing with oil. Nowadays the stress is on the hands, which were in fact only a symbol of prayer dedicated to the person in question.

As to who did this, we know that the bishop presided at the laying on of hands, but he could hardly have been present when women were washed, and in fact both women and men were clothed in white after their washing and then taken to the bishop, who seems to have been in another room. The place of baptism varied according to the water supply. Where people washed in streams, Christians were baptized in streams, but in towns with public bath-houses they probably rented these, and in large churches built their own bath-houses. Where remains exist they show basins where the candidates would stand up to ankles or knees in water and have more water poured over them. There was not enough depth for their being completely submerged, and that was not customary in Greek baths anyway, but it probably happened in some outdoor baptisms, and possibly indoors as well.

As to who were baptized, Tertullian objected to baptizing children, which shows it must have been done, and it seems to have been the regular if not the universal custom. There was a lengthy period of preparation, during which candidates were only admitted to the first part of Sunday worship. Baptism tended to be restricted to the evening before Easter, since it was a symbolic passing through the Red Sea waters.

But all this became more difficult when the bishop ceased to be in every congregation and might be miles away. In the West the sacrament was split by time, in the East it was split by place. The Western Christian received the washing part in infancy, and on being old enough to undertake the promises was then 'confirmed' by the bishop, receiving the laying on of hands with anointing for the gift of the Holy Spirit. Of course this assumed a bishop who would or could cover his whole area at regular intervals, and in fact most were admitted to holy communion long before being confirmed, and many were never confirmed at all. Eastern Christians received baptism of washing as infants, this being more than the symbolic pouring of water in the West, but immersion in a font, and in the same ceremony they also received confirmation with oils – but without the laying on of hands. In theory the bishop is still the minister of this sacrament, since he has consecrated the oils, even though he is separated from the infant by anything up to a thousand miles. Whether it is better to split the sacrament by time or by space is a matter of philosophy, though in certain types of physics they are the same thing anyway, but the experts are usually concerned with not putting asunder that which God has joined together. They want a single ceremony, but except for adult converts it cannot be done. Nor is this just because the bishop is a long way away; the real problem is leaving something to be linked to an actual profession of faith when the child has reached years of discernment, if not of discretion. The profession of faith cannot be ignored, or should not be ignored. Present day baptisms and confirmations may be a bit illogical and they are not the usage of the early church, but we are not living in the early church.

The Sunday service was the eucharist which is holy communion or the mass or the Lord's Supper. There is no evidence of any exceptions to this practice, but there probably were exceptions, and there is no reason why the universal custom of the early church should be binding forever. True, Sunday was the day of the resurrection, and of the eucharist, and without a eucharist it would not have been Sunday, but there was nothing written down (so far as we know) even about having a Sunday every week. For most of Christian history the custom of having the eucharist every week has only been maintained by lay people not receiving holy communion at it. Whether this is better than not having a eucharist on some Sundays is arguable. This is something which the church must decide in the light of the Holy Spirit.

The first part of the eucharist was instructive. There was a short prayer called a 'collect' for reasons now forgotten; this varied from Sunday to Sunday and something of their force has been lost in translation. There were then readings from an epistle and from a gospel, with a psalm separating them. From the fourth century these became fixed, though nobody knows on what basis. There are relics of a scheme of reading an entire epistle or gospel through week after week, but only relics. There was no obvious connection between what came from the epistle and what came from the gospel, and when in the eighth century Charlemagne wanted copies of Roman extracts from epistles and gospels to standardize usage throughout his realms, the front page of one of the two books got rubbed off (supposedly while crossing the Alps) so if there had been any common theme before there was none after that.

Noted bishops explained the meanings of what had been read, and these sermons still exist, but it is not certain how the less-educated bishops of smaller towns, or even less-educated priests, looked upon preaching. In an age when oratory was much prized they may have taken to it naturally, but they may have thought it not part of their job-description. Yet there was certainly a good deal of preaching, though it eventually died out, and modern preaching is said to have begun again with instructions given in the nave of the church during the Middle Ages.

After the un-baptized had withdrawn, and there were places and times when this happened even before the gospel was read, there came the offering of bread and wine, and a long prayer which was basically a thanksgiving, from which the Greek name 'eucharist' was taken. There was a reading of the words from the Last Supper as recorded in the gospels, and there was an offering of the consecrated elements of bread and wine. They were then received as the Body and Blood of Christ, though philosophical definitions of this last were only to come somewhat later. There was probably also a prayer that the Holy Spirit might descend upon the bread and wine, which became particularly important in the East. But there was also a prayer that the sacrifice might be taken to the altar on high – that is, that the sacrifice here might be united to the sacrifice of Christ on the cross which was offered for eternity in heaven. This downward or upward movement might lead to downward or upward views of the Christian life.

At about the year 150 Justin Martyr wrote of the eucharist at Rome: 'There is then brought to the president bread and a cup of wine mixed with water; and he, taking them, offers up praise and glory to the Father of the universe, through the name of the Son and the Holy Ghost, and gives thanks at considerable length for our being counted worthy to receive these things at his hands ... those who are called by us deacons give to each of those present to partake ... and to those who are absent they carry away a portion ... For not as common bread and common drink do we receive these; but in like manner as Jesus Christ our Saviour, having been made flesh by the word of God, had both flesh and blood for our salvation, so likewise have we been taught that the food which is blessed by the word of prayer transmitted from him, and by which our blood and flesh by assimilation are nourished, is the flesh and blood of that Jesus who was made flesh.' Fifty years later Hippolytus of Rome provided a similar account, stating that some who presided might prepare their own prayers for the eucharist, but others, presumably less gifted, would use a fixed form, of which his example was in the tradition still widely used today.

Creeds, or statements of faith, began in baptism then spread elsewhere. Hippolytus has the presbyter saying to the candidate, 'Dost thou believe in God the Father almighty?', to which the reply is, 'I believe', and the candidate is baptized the first time. Then, 'Dost thou believe in Christ Jesus, the Son of God, who was born by the Holy Ghost of the Virgin Mary, and was crucified under Pontius Pilate, and was dead and buried, and rose again the third day, alive from the dead, and ascended into heaven, and sat at the right hand of the Father, and will come to judge the quick and the dead?' The candidate again replies, 'I believe', and is baptized again. Then, 'Dost thou believe in the Holy Ghost, in the holy Church, and the resurrection of the flesh?' For the third time the reply is, 'I believe', and the candidate is baptized for the last time.

This is roughly what we now call the Apostles' Creed, and it was Western and less elaborate than the form used in the East, which is now called the Nicene Creed. This is said to have come from Jerusalem, and was later enlarged to include the 'one substance' teaching of the council of Nicaea and the council of Constantinople, but it was originally a baptismal creed, as can be seen from its beginning 'I believe in God ...' and not 'We believe in God ...'. But modern forms often do begin 'We believe in God ...', partly because the years in which worship was re-ordered, from 1960 until 1980, were also years in which individualism was out of favour, and the 'People of God' were in favour, but partly because it was supposed that a Nicene Creed must have begun at Nicaea and the bishops must have said 'We ...' In fact the bishops at Nicaea gave their assent to something much shorter, but this did get mixed up with the older baptismal creed, so it does not much matter whether it begins 'I' or 'We'.

Of course these creeds were still only used at baptism, and it is not quite clear when Easterners began to use their creed after the gospel in the eucharist. This was then copied by Westerners, who did not use their own creed then, but the Eastern or Nicene one – ending up in the ridiculous situation of having one creed for the eucharist and another for baptism or any other occasion. Finally, some modern baptismal forms have been given body by having the relic of the first part (and the most primitive part) of the eucharistic prayer, beginning 'Lift up your hearts ...', incorporated into them. It has been observed that if the statement of faith, which lay at the centre of baptism, has been taken over by the eucharist, it is only fair that the central thanksgiving of the eucharist should likewise be misappropriated by the service of baptism.

Daily services appear to have been based on Jewish use of the psalms and readings, with special emphasis on Wednesday, Friday, and Saturday. These services were developed by monks but it is not clear how many ordinary Christians were able or willing to be present. It is equally unclear how many Christians followed the advice of their leaders to begin and end each act of their day with prayer; official statements of what people ought to do are more often evidence that they are not doing it than that they are.

Singing seems to have been common from earliest times; psalms were sung as they had been in Jewish life, and specifically Christian hymns can be found embedded in the New Testament itself. There was a rapid growth of church music in the fourth century, when special choirs were formed. A major factor in this was the construction of large churches in which singing was necessary if the bishop was to be heard clearly at the back, and singing was necessary if the congregation were to say the same things at the same time. But if the purpose of church music was practical, it had the additional advantage of occasionally being of such quality as to provide pleasure to the listener. Indeed, this is still the case today.

Speaking-in-tongues, or 'glossalalia', was associated with the Montanist movement in Asia Minor, though it is not certain that this is what they did. Montanus himself is said to have prophesied in 172, as did two women associates, but there was a rejection of the wider church which led to the condemnation of the movement. However, it is possible and perhaps probable that there were other times and places in the long history of the early church in which there was speaking-in-tongues without it being condemned or even particularly noted. Some modern observers have noted the high profile of female prophets in the movement, and have concluded that the Montanists were either fervent feminists or relics of an early Christianity in which there was no bias against women. It is more likely that their prophets were mainly female on the assumption that the female mind had less in it to obstruct the free passage of messages from the beyond.

Finally, Christian worship was shaped by its surroundings. The first Christians seem to have met in private houses, and if the congregation outgrew such places it might move to a cattle-shed or warehouse. But even before official toleration it became usual for a special structure to be bought or built in the larger centres, and if these were not hidden they were not conspicuous either. The shape was that of the Roman public building, oblong with a semi-circular apse at one end. In the apse would be the bishop's chair, which was the main article of furniture before the altar became dominant. A rail would fence off the altar from the congregation, and another fence off the unbaptized. There would probably be a stand on which the sacred texts could be supported, and those texts were not rolls of parchment but books in the modern style, of pages piled one on another. This might have meant that Christians had direct access to small bits of their scriptures and did not see these as a constantly unfolding narrative, with deep consequences for Christian theology, but it might also have meant nothing at all. Returning to furnishings, there could be chairs for presbyters and even for the infirm. The baptistry, if there was one, would be separate, for reasons of modesty.

All of which was light-years away from the sacrifices offered to pagan statues. Robin Lane Fox has written that the principle characteristic of pagan devotion was 'an east-facing aspect, bathed in the dawn', and this could be and was incorporated into Christianity. But he also notes that 'pagan cities were crammed with forests of statuary', which was rejected by the Christians who followed the Jews by thinking of God in terms of words and pure light, rather than of a visual design. As the Book of Revelation put it, God is 'like a precious stone, blazing in brilliant red and white'. Yet a God for all must appear to all, and that meant Greeks as well as Jews. Christian worship was to take in statues and icons and very much more, including customs which are only just bursting upon us.

9

Origen

'Who could ever read everything that Origen wrote?' Nobody, but if it comes down to it, he did not write it anyway. He had converted a wealthy man named Ambrose who showed his gratitude by providing him with seven stenographers, plus copyists – in fact, his own publishing house. And the words flowed forth and forth and forth.

There are two stories about Origen which every student knows, and if they are not true then they have been making the rounds for so long that there is nothing we can do about it. The first is that in 202, when he would have been about seventeen years old, his father died in persecution at Alexandria in Egypt, and Origen would have rushed out to give his life also had not his mother hidden his clothes. The second is that he castrated himself in a youthful attempt to fulfil the commands of the gospel, real or imagined. Modern scholars seem to think this did actually happen, though it is hard to imagine the reasoning behind it when the personality of Origen is taken into account.

Be that as it may or may not, he succeeded Clement as head of the catechetical school at Alexandria, soaked himself in philosophy, and taught a way into Christianity through Platonism. His fame spread, as did his writings, and if we do not have those writings today, that is because a variety of his teachings or supposed teachings were condemned as 'Origenism' after his death and most copies of his work destroyed. He was never without enemies, though he tried to avoid bitterness or anger in his work. And one of his enemies was the Bishop Demetrius.

Demetrius seems to have been suspicious of any sort of intellectual activity, and was certainly suspicious of the most famous Christian in Alexandria. When Origen went to Palestine and preached, while only a layman, this was taken as a breach of good manners. In 230 he went on another visit to Palestine where he was ordained priest, which caused Demetrius to exile him and deprive him of his post in the school. The reason may have been that Origen was a resident of Alexandria rather than Palestine, or that his having been castrated barred him from ordination, or it may have been something else. The result was that Origen continued his literary and teaching work in Caesarea or Palestine.

Origen's thought is not put forward in logical order, but in a great many statements, some of which can only be understood when opposed by others of his statements. As with so many great thinkers, we are not so much looking at the final product of his thought as joining with him in the search for truth. No single quotation will give his full judgment on any single issue, and if we are to know his mind it is necessary to read more deeply than most of us can ever hope to do. And he did not define his terms. This, and the fact that he never really completed his thoughts, but rather dragged the reader along with him, has left him open to charges of heresy. It is said that these were unfair since they related to matters which were only defined long after his death, and which were still open questions in his day, but the problem goes deeper than that. Origen was not making theology; he was making theologians.

Origen did not accept the view of Clement of Alexandria that philosophy was to the Greeks what the Old Testament was to the Jews. He was much more careful about philosophy, but he used it nonetheless, and what he used was Plato. And the Plato he used said that the things of this world have ideals in another, and Christianity is a pilgrimage from the worldly to the ideal or the spiritual. Which may be Plato, and yet it is the sort of thing which could occur, and has occurred, to many others. However, it does lead to the belief that the opposite of truth is not falsehood but the mere symbol of truth, while sin is accepting the symbol and going no further. On the other hand, and this may be a reaction against the Gnostics, true knowledge is not something intellectual but a union with the ideal, and a mingling with the ideal, and in the end it is love. All of which is quite proper and orthodox, but it could lead to confusion, and it did.

On the Bible, Origen tried to find a middle way between the literal meaning and the symbolic, but he is best known for his defence of symbolic teaching. He argued that the literal sense is the source of the spiritual sense, and only so can the Old Testament be understood. Everything in the Old Testament could be used in this way, with enough inspiration and imagination, and in Origen's hands the most tiresome lists of rules were discovered to be clues to deep spiritual truths. He would have found spiritual meaning in a computer manual. Yet his method was basically right. The New Testament is full of symbolic language, and just because some things are to be taken at face value, it does not mean that other things are. But to use symbolic language means that the things used as symbols, that is the creation, must be regarded as good – or they could not carry a spiritual message. Origen was battling with those who rejected the goodness of creation and went to the extreme of literalism which demanded that God has real hands and a real voice. And he was also arguing for the free will of the biblical writers, against the view that God dictated everything and they wrote in a trance. But his view of symbols linked them closely to the things symbolized – he insisted that words were essentially descriptive, like 'thud' or 'staccato'.

His doctrine of God was as elusive and many-sided as his doctrine of everything else. There is an essential masculinity in God, seen in the view, as put forward by Henri Crouzel, that 'in the presence of God and his Christ, every human soul is feminine, Wife and Mother'. But if the Father is almighty, he is not beyond response, and perhaps in some sense even changes, when faced with the plight of his people. He does weep for sinners, and his delight is with the sons of men, and if this is contradictory, so be it. And the Father is united with the Son; the idea of the Son being born of the Father is all right as far as it goes, but the use of human relationships to illustrate the nature of God can never be final.

The Son is born of the Father but never separated from him, and the birth of the Son from the Father goes on forever. As for the humanity and divinity of Christ, the humanity is described as a screen, hiding his divinity. And yet it is also the means by which his divinity is revealed. Nonetheless, it is true, as Rowan Williams has argued, that for Origen, 'Christ is less than fully incarnate', and there is 'a general unconcern with the human will and human development of Jesus – a sharp contrast with Irenaeus'.

'The Bride looks for the Bridegroom who, after showing himself, has disappeared,' wrote Origen in one of his rare personal revelations. 'Often, God is my witness, I have felt that the Bridegroom was approaching, and that he was as near as possible to me; then he has suddenly gone away.' This will have a familiar ring to anyone who has made the least shift to progress in the spiritual life, but on another subject, the dart and the wound of love, Origen was making an original contribution. Yet that contribution is lost to us – it has degenerated into the sort of thing which is found on St Valentine's Day cards. The symbol has become so commonplace that it ceases to be a symbol of anything higher. We are on solider ground when we follow Origen's belief that the more you trust in the spiritual the more you understand it.

As for the creation, he taught that it took place out of time, co-created with the endless generation or birth of the Son, and there were possible successive worlds, which, like souls, existed before the world which we know. And this brings us to his doctrine of the soul.

He believed in the pre-existence of the soul; this is immensely important to the modern world where a belief in pre-existence of souls, consciously held or only assumed, may well be a factor in opposing contraception. Put bluntly, if there are souls waiting for bodies, it is sinful to prevent those bodies coming into existence. But Origen's way of reaching this belief was ingenious. Instead of taking the first two chapters of Genesis as alternative creation stories (many Christians have not even realized that there is more than one creation story), Origen held that the first chapter concerned the creation of the soul, in the image of God, and the second concerned the creation of the body, which does not have the image of God. It can only have this image if it is joined to a pre-existent soul. Since souls existed before there was a fall, they were involved in it, though not to the same extent as demons, and were, as Crouzel puts it, 'judged fit by God to replenish the human race'. But Origen was unwilling to commit himself to the method by which the soul enters the body.

'In regard to the soul, whether it takes its rise from the transference of the seed ... or whether it has some other beginning ... all this is not very clearly defined in the teaching.' In fact nothing is very clearly defined in the teaching when we are dealing with Origen, and some would say with any other theologian, but we can see what he is driving at. He is using Plato, and the soul is nearer the reality than is the body. But there are problems in doing this; Origen had to argue that between death and resurrection the soul had some sort of bodily shell, or else it would have been entirely spiritual, and thus the ideal, and so God. And in all this Origen was opposing popular ideas that the soul was in fact the blood, which in refined form was the seed. If this were so the soul would die with the body and rest in the cemetery until the day of resurrection, and this would partly explain the digging of elaborate graves such as the catacombs of Rome.

Our free will is linked to the nature of the soul. And it is not surprising that Origen, with his high view of the creation, should have had a strong view of free will. But he was also moved to oppose pagan astrology which, after the moral murkiness of pagan myths, had swung to a view of human life in which all was fated by the stars. It was to protect free will that Origen argued against universal salvation; people had to have a chance of damnation to choose to be saved.

But since sexual activity is of this world, and therefore of the symbol and not the ideal, it represented impurity even within marriage. And Origen may well have been the first to teach the perpetual virginity of the Virgin Mary, she being the pattern of virginity amongst women as Jesus was amongst men. Another first for Origen seems to have been his teaching that paradise is immediately available upon death, which is hard to reconcile with his other teachings. He also argued that the risen body of Christ was not as it had been before death, but glorified. And this was, of course, extended to all Christians, whose risen bodies should not be as they had been before death. This is a lively issue today; never does Easter come round without television interviewers roaming the face of the earth to discover what clerics believe in the 'bodily resurrection', their assumption being that resurrection of the body must be bodily, or physical, instead of spiritual, by which they mean merely symbolical. Which, of course, is the opposite of Origen's belief. But Origen went too far in separating life in heaven from that on earth. He argued that there would be no need for human relationships on earth to be continued in heaven, and that organs and limbs which were only needed on earth would not be found on glorified bodies in heaven. His opponents asked if these would be cubic or spherical.

Origen held that martyrdom was the supreme baptism, the washing not with water but with blood, and he even regretted that under Philip the Arabian there was no persecution of Christians. But with Decius as emperor, and with Origen being the most famous of all Christian scholars, he was imprisoned and tortured. He endured 'chains and bodily torments, agony in iron and the darkness of his cell, for days on end his legs were pulled four paces apart in the torturers' stocks ...'. He survived the end of the persecution, but never fully recovered, and died around the year 254. A thousand years later pilgrims were still visiting what was thought to be his tomb, moved to a cathedral in Acre, but in due course the cathedral vanished and so did the tomb. Yet his teaching survived in the thoughts and words of countless successors, until it was said that he was the father of all orthodoxy and of all heresy. Sometimes in the same person.

10

Ministry

'He did not write a book.' So trumpeted an archbishop, as only archbishops can, before the consecration of a bishop. The 'he' of his sermon was Jesus Christ, and he meant that Christ had not given his followers a book but had instead given them a church, of which the ministry was part, and a most important part. Other Christians, and perhaps even other archbishops, would have said that Christ did not quite write a book but arranged for it to be done, and the ministry was really just a happy way in which to explain and re-enact what was in that book.

Obviously these two views, and the countless views between them, will lead to different views of the ministry. If the church is what matters, then the church is our link to the days of the apostles, but if the book is what matters, that is our link to the days of the apostles. And this is 'apostolic succession'; all Christians believe that they are following in the footsteps of the apostles, and all Christians believe that there is apostolic succession. They differ in the extent that it is to be found in a body of people on the one hand, or in a set of ideas on the other. And it is right that they should differ. Different ages and societies must have different interpretations if they are all to be linked to what the apostles did and the apostles taught.

Unfortunately, almost any group of Christians assumes that the ministry of the early church must reflect that group's view of the ministry in their own day. If they claim that they have a particular form of ministry because the early church did, they more often believe that the early church had such a form of ministry because they themselves have it. If they have no ministry because they have specified nothing for ministers to do, they also believe that the early church had none, and it developed long afterwards in a period of corruption. If they believe that all Christians are ministers in all ways, they believe this was the original pattern. If they have bishops, they believe these were to be found in the early church, though there may be differences as to whether these were essential or not. If they do not have bishops, they believe that the early church had none. But almost all churches claim to be as the apostles were. Christianity is based on what happened, and cannot get away from it, and rarely tries to do so.

Having said all this, the evidence from early times is over-whelming, and it is its meaning which is in doubt. We begin with apostles who are thought to have moved about, though there is no evidence that most of them did anything at all. The individual congregation had a bishop (the word means 'overseer') and presbyters (the word means 'elders') and deacons. The bishop presided at the eucharist, and probably did most of the preaching, while the presbyters were the committee to look after the build-ing, if they had one, and whatever else troubled Christians of those days. Deacons were servants, and it is often unclear if they were church servants or personal servants of the bishops. It has been suggested that some of them may have been slaves. When deacons were ordained it was by the bishop alone, since they were his servants, while presbyters were ordained by other presbyters, including the bishop, though more about this later. It may be argued that all this ministry came from Jewish sources, or from Greek, but someone to take the chair and someone to be on a committee and someone to sweep the floor is so nearly universal in human history that we do not have to find any particular origin for it.

The big question is whether the bishop was a jumped-up presbyter or a successor to the apostles. The answer to this question will depend more on whether we share the views of the archbishop quoted at the start of this chapter, or the alternative set of views, than it will depend on the facts available. There are some for whom the mere idea that a bishop was a successor to the apostles is a blasphemous suggestion that scripture is inadequate. There are others for whom the suggestion that the ministry of the church is not related to the apostles means that Christianity is not a living faith rooted in a people, but just a set of principles never made flesh.

As for the facts, it is clear that some, such as Irenaeus, held a strong doctrine of apostolic succession in bishops, though the emphasis, natural in an argument against heresy, was on their teaching rather than their consecration. Then there was Ignatius of Antioch, he of the wrenching of bones, who went to his death writing, 'Follow, all of you, the bishop, as Jesus Christ followed the Father, and follow the presbytery as the apostles.' For Ignatius bishops were everything, and to say that this was just because local heretics in Asia Minor were going against their bishops is not very convincing. You cannot discount a belief just because it is used in times when it is needed. (Or you and I cannot do this; many historians do it every day.) On the other hand, Hippolytus of Rome was very Presbyterian and took a dim view of bishops, but he was rather embittered at losing out in an election to be bishop. Jerome managed to be embittered without ever having been in an election at all, but his main complaint was that deacons were getting out of hand. 'For when the apostle plainly teaches that presbyters and bishops are the same, what happens to the server of tables and widows that he sets himself up arrogantly over those at whose prayers the body and blood of Christ are made?' He then argues, as did others, that bishops at Alexandria had once been consecrated by presbyters and not by other bishops, which may well have been true, and finally throws away this card by saying, 'For, with the exception of ordaining, what does a bishop do which a presbyter does not?'

It is sometimes said that bishop and presbyter mean the same thing, but they obviously do not. They are different words with different meanings. It may be that they mean the same people, but that is not the same thing at all. And if they mean the same people, it is recognized that all bishops are presbyters, but this does not necessarily mean that all presbyters are bishops. There were those in the early church who minimized the distinctions, and others who went in the other direction, but when it comes to what they did we are left with the overall impression that bishops were not just jumped-up presbyters but something more. If there were exceptions, and there almost certainly were, they were exceptions.

However, this leaves us with Jerome's presbyters doing everything that a bishop did except ordain. That was not the primitive pattern. How did the member of the local committee move from counting the collection to presiding at the eucharist? The conventional answer is that somewhere between the years 80 and 180 the church suddenly expanded at such a rate that new congregations were formed and the presbyters were sent out to look after these. Meanwhile, the bishop kept his chair in the old central church, now called a cathedral after the Greek word *cathedra* meaning chair. But this answer will not wash. If there was expansion, it would have been more logical to keep the old pattern of a presbyter who did not lead worship, and a bishop who did, and simply multiply the number of bishops with presbyters and deacons. Something else must have been involved. It may have been a pre-occupation of bishops with heresies and other matters which took them out of their congregations, or it may have been a demand by presbyters that they play a wider part in church life. Or, horror of horrors, it may have been that presbyters always were more involved in worship than we have believed, and bishop and presbyter were not that far apart. But presbyters were now clearly seen to be be presiding at the eucharist, and once that was more clearly considered to be a sacrifice they were seen to be offering a sacrifice. And so the shortened form of presbyter, 'priest', was used to mean an offerer of a sacrifice, in Christian or other religions. Until then the proper Latin word for such a person, 'sacerdos', had been used for the bishop alone.

But what about deacons? In the West, but not in the East, the deacon gradually faded out of the picture, though the name was kept alive for those who would be priests and who had to pass through a whole string of lesser ranks, readers and doorkeepers and sub-deacons and deacons, before reaching the real thing. This has meant that countless church reformers have believed that if there was a missing ingredient in the modern church, something which existed in scripture and in the early church, and which guaranteed success, that must be the deacon. Once the deacon is restored, then all will be well. And rather half-hearted attempts have been made to restore deacons, but nobody really wants them once they have them. There is nothing that they can do in the age of the vacuum cleaner.

As for why they faded away, this is still a mystery. There are grumbles from various people, of whom we have noted Jerome at the end of the fourth century, and might have noted the council of Nicaea in 325, about deacons getting out of hand. They were servants, yet they were putting themselves above the presbyters, who were skilled wine-skin makers and used-chariot salesmen. And they were trying to get elected to be bishops. There was a real danger that the deacons, who represented nobody, would use their closeness to elderly bishops to take their place. Deacons were soon wearing the bishops' cast off clothes, or just bishops' livery, and these have since become the accepted vestments of the deacon. And when the bishop was too doddery to read the gospel, his deacon would do it for him, and this became the work of the deacon. In fact deacons were ordained before the reading of the gospel, since all ministers were ordained at that part of the service where they were needed. It is only in the present generation that deacons have been ordained with bishops and priests at the offering of bread and wine. Whether a person ordained at that point of the service is really a deacon may be doubted, but it does not matter. Deacons do not matter.

If deacons do not matter, do deaconesses? If deacons were the servants of the early bishops, and bishops then had servants just as they now have word-processors and food-processors and gadgets for opening their garage doors, there would have been female servants as well as male. But if the male servant who was the equivalent of the word-processor figured in the bishop's public ministry, the female servant who was the equivalent of the food-processor did not. (The gadgets for opening garage-doors have only been introduced into this paragraph to show that, in the early church as now, there were grey areas in both sexuality and ministry.) There would thus be no need for her to be brought into her work by laying on of hands with prayer, and yet we know that in at least some places, notably Rome as described by Hippolytus, deaconesses were ordained as were deacons. This was probably because there were two things in the early church which could only be done by women. Baptisms of women were patterned on washings of women in the public baths, and for this the deaconess was the equivalent of the female bath attendant. Again, women prevented by age or illness from attending church would have the eucharistic elements brought to them, and pagan husbands, or even Christian husbands, might frown on male visitors. So the bishop's female servants became servants of the church as well as of the bishop, and yet any woman serving in ministry was contrary to the normal view of women and that may be why deaconesses died out. At the Council of Nicaea it was decreed that since deaconesses had not received the laying on of hands, and probably most had not, they were to be counted as laywomen. The other female order was that of widows, and they seem to have been tolerated on the grounds that they were sexually extinct and thus hardly women at all.

Moving on to presbyters, the sixteenth century saw the birth of Presbyterianism. Its main feature was government by a system of church courts, with no interference by the state in church affairs, though with a good deal of interference by the church in state affairs. The second feature was that there was only one order of ministers, presbyters or elders, though these were later divided between 'preaching elders' and 'ruling elders'. In theory the 'preaching elder' was the presbyter-bishop of ancient times, but the mediaeval bishop was rejected, partly because he had been very much a state officer as well as a churchman.

But Presbyterianism is not vocal about its theory today. If there is opposition to the idea of a bishop this is because bishops are regarded as undemocratic, though rule solely by two types of elders can hardly be called democratic, and in fact nobody in the sixteenth century was or wanted to be democratic. Yet the system works in practice, and the theory has crept into Anglicanism, which has now swung from state-appointed bishops to a system of synods or church courts which is far more Presbyterian than Anglican in ethos. And Roman Catholics in the Second Vatican Council of the 1960s adopted the idea, if not the fact, of rule by a College of Bishops – Collegiality. It is Presbyterianism without the involvement of presbyters. In fact, the idea of Presbyterianism is flourishing throughout the world, except amongst Presbyterians.

Finally, bishops. They were presbyters, but they were also linked with bishops in other communities. A bishop was normally consecrated by other bishops, and not by the presbyters of his own church. Bishops in the same area met together for common action, and bishops wrote to one another. In due course each civil province had an archbishop, and in due course the Roman empire saw bishops as the focal points of church life on which to apply pressure. Bishops walked the tightrope between serving the state and serving the church, though some were so powerful that no state could be indifferent to them. Later history produced endless complications; in sixteenth-century Ireland there were even a few bishops who held one diocese from Henry VIII, and another diocese from the Pope.

But if this is the general picture, there are those who would argue that there never was any real structure in the early church, and should be none now. This view was supported when a document known to scholars but lost, the Didache ('didakay', or teaching), came to light in 1873. It was found in a Jerusalem monastery by a Greek archbishop who had it published, whereupon it aroused such controversy that many wished it had been left where it was. The Didache is in two parts; the first is on morals, and may go back as far as the years 70 or 90, while the second is on church order and is more often dated around 150. And on church order it implied that teachers and prophets were more important than bishops and deacons, while presbyters were never mentioned at all.

This pleased many Christians of that period, who leaned towards the sort of religion in which nobody was very sinful so a sacrifice for sin was not all that important, while education would do almost everything. In their view, the early Christians were followers of a teacher and put the emphasis on teachers and prophets, not bishops and deacons. As if that was not enough, the lack of reference to presbyters meant they were the same people as the bishops. And in the rather detailed instructions on how to preside at the eucharist and what prayers to use, there is a phrase, 'suffer the prophets to give thanks as much as they will ...', which might mean that anyone with prophetic gifts could preside at the eucharist, whether ordained or not.

Or it might mean something else. That a bishop who had prophetic gifts was not bound to a particular set of words, though others were. And if the teachers and prophets were clearly on top, the Didache was trying to curb their power, and increase that of the bishops and deacons, for 'they also minister unto you the ministry of the prophets and teachers ...' And if there was no mention of presbyters, that was because they had no special part in worship. And the directions for fasting and baptism and the eucharist were very specific. The Didache could be used to prove either case, and it was, and it is.

Lastly, there is apostolic succession. It has been argued that all Christians believe in apostolic succession, unless they reject the apostles. The question is how. Is it by a set of doctrines, or by a set of people? Or do the two support each other? There are extremists who say that apostolic succession should be a matter of doctrine and nothing else, and that Christianity can spread just by a Bible left on a desert island, though this rarely happens. There are those who say that it is the continuing life of the church with its ministry from the beginning which is essential. But really there should be both – a continuing church, the body of Christ, with the faith of Christ. Neither can exist without the other. When Irenaeus listed bishops who went back to the apostles, these were bishops who taught the true faith. And the true faith is that God was in Christ, and that faith was written on hearts and not on tablets.

If this is the central issue, the argument between bishops and presbyters is a working out of that issue. There are Presbyterians with a high doctrine of ministry who argue that apostolic succession in the ministry is necessary or at least important, but it is through presbyters. They would reject the view that if you have the right faith then you can create a ministry from nothing. In fact there are few Christians who would want to do this, even if many would say it could be done in times of crisis. Congregationalists believe in a congregation ordaining its own minister but this may still be, and usually is, a form of apostolic succession. As for apostolic succession through bishops, that is a lesser matter, but this is and probably always will be the major and almost normative form of the succession of the ministry.

Yet all this talk of bishops will appear unreal to the Congregationalist or, since Congregationalists have largely moved into unions with others, to Baptists. There the picture is of the independent congregation with a minister surrounded by elders and deacons – which is very much the picture of the bishop with presbyters and deacons in the early church. This has been deliberately adopted as the ministry of the New Testament, and the underlying view is that Christians should take the pattern directly from the New Testament and not from something which has grown haphazardly since New Testament times. For growth since New Testament times is assumed to have been haphazard. Basically, the argument is whether the New Testament produced the church, or the church produced the New Testament. 'He did not write a book.' Or did he? The answer is clear. He did and he didn't.

11

Grace

It is commonly said that Christians of Western Europe are practical, while Christians of Eastern Europe are spiritual and deep into theological speculation. There is not much truth to this. The Easterners can be as practical as any when they have to, and the Westerners can be as theological as any when it takes their fancy. That the doctrines of the Trinity and of the Person of Christ were mainly worked out in the East is true, and that the West largely looked on is also true, but there then came a great heresy in which the East merely looked on while the West fought it out. It concerned Grace. And it was essentially a re-play of the old questions of the Trinity and the Person of Christ. If those were trying to find a middle ground between the idea that humanity was good, and the idea that humanity was bad, so was the argument over Grace.

It began with a strange character named Pelagius who came from Britain or thereabouts. He was a big man both vertically and horizontally, supposedly through eating porridge. He was of high moral character and an exponent of high moral character. Even Augustine, who opposed his views, refused to attack him directly because he respected his integrity. It is usual to regard Pelagians as not taking sin seriously, and therefore not taking the need for a saviour as seriously as they should. Their concern was with the dignity and freedom of human nature; they started from the human and not from God. But Pelagius never took sin lightly; it was the appallingly sinful Christians of his day that caused his concern for moral reform. And, while Pelagius probably did slip into heresy as the argument went on, the real heretics were others and Pelagius eventually dropped out of the argument altogether.

'Thou commandest chastity – grant what thou commandest, and command what thou wilt,' Augustine had written, and it was this passage which horrified Pelagius who felt that, taken on its own, it denied free will. He was probably right. If God could and did command whatever he wanted and then force it on people, those people were not free and could not be blamed if they did not do good. It was the fault of God who had not forced chastity or some other virtue upon them. And Pelagius saw it as a matter of moral character. Augustine was willing to do this, but his main concern was elsewhere. If God is God, then he must be able to enforce his will. He cannot be limited, like a joint stock company. He is absolute and sovereign. Once that was established, Augustine would have gone on to make some allowances for free will, but the freedom of God, the complete freedom of God, came first. And in this he was right, even if he was so set on establishing the freedom of God that he never really did much for human freedom.

The argument was worked out in a series of voyages across the Mediterranean; no heresy in Christian history has involved as much sea-air. And, for those with a social conscience, so much work by galley slaves. First of all, Pelagius arrived in Rome around the year 400, with a friend named Caelestius. In 409, just before Rome fell to the barbarians, they both moved on, Caelestius going to Carthage where he promptly got into trouble with African church leaders. The heresy which was now associated with both men, but perhaps only held in its fullness by Caelestius, was that a human being could live without sinning, that there was no such thing as original sin, that the sin of Adam and Eve was personal and only applied to them, that grace is not essential though it is a good thing to have, and that human beings have free will. Obviously not all these statements have the same force. The first, that a human being could live without sinning, is a rather extreme statement of the happy view of humanity, but it is not really over the edge into heresy. The Pelagians used Job as a biblical example of being free from sin, but this relied on a very literal view of the Old Testament and did not cut much ice. To say that there is no original sin, by which was meant something more than a basic tendency to sin in human nature, was to deny the social nature of the human race, and thus of salvation. But it was whether grace was necessary which came to be the main point in later argument.

Caelestius in Carthage was asked why infants were baptized if there was no original sin, and he gave evasive answers. Or perhaps they only seemed evasive; Caelestius was legally trained and yet rather impetuous, and his theology was sometimes not all that clear. Here there was a sharp difference of emphasis between Pelagius and Caelestius; the former was a moral reformer, and the latter was concerned about baptism. Pelagius tended to argue that baptism was not so much a washing of sin but a gift of higher sanctification in Christ, what would now be called 'Second Baptism'. Caelestius was concerned to preserve God from a charge of sinfulness by arguing that sin comes solely from humanity, and until the human will is exercised there can be no sin. This was to weaken the solidarity of the human race, and behind it there may very well have been a relic of the old argument of the origin of the souls. We tend to look at all this argument in terms of whether God damns people to hell before they are born, which is a matter of where the soul goes, but it may be that this depended on where the soul comes from. Caelestius seems to have had a view of infants born into sealed containers, where nobody could influence them, while his opponents had a view of them receiving everything from their parents and their surroundings. And 'everything' included their souls.

Anyway, Caelestius was expelled from Africa. Augustine then stated that if there had been no fall of humanity into sin then Christ would not have come. This was denied by Duns Scotus in the Middle Ages, but whether Christ would have come to earth if no salvation were necessary is a somewhat difficult question for human beings to answer with any certainty. Augustine then went on to say that infants dying without baptism were condemned, which may be logical, but is not sensible. This created a storm in Carthage when he said it. The next event was a certain well-bred lady named Demetrias taking the veil and asking everyone for advice. Pelagius and Augustine took the opportunity to argue with one another over her head. After reading Augustine's advice, certain Sicilian supporters of Pelagius remarked that 'If sin cannot be avoided, then it is not sin; if it can be avoided, then man can be without sin.'

At this point a zealot named Paulus Orosius, who had left Spain just ahead of the Vandal invaders, arrived in Palestine where Pelagius had been well received by the local church, though attacked by a Western translator of the Old Testament named Jerome. Since Jerome was scarcely the sort of person who would make friends if he could avoid it, his condemnation of Pelagius did not impress the locals. They supported Pelagius at a synod in Diospolis where he had put his case in the mildest form possible. Orosius then sailed off to Rome, where in 416 he put the matter before Pope Innocent I who condemned Pelagius but said, perhaps as an exercise in tact, that he could not make out what had been said at Diospolis, and that Rome was the final authority – which it certainly was in a case concerning Westerners.

Next year Innocent died and was succeeded by one Zozimus who said that Pelagius and Caelestius were orthodox. For this he has gone down in history as a fool. But Innocent had said he did not know what was decided at Diospolis, and Zozimus knew that Pelagius' accusers included two disgraced bishops from the West. Finally, he held that the essentials of the faith were the traditional matters of Trinity and the Person of Christ, while differences on the question of grace had never been a matter of heresy. But the Africans were soon up in arms over this, and Zozimus managed to imply that Pelagius and Caelestius were not orthodox but that his earlier statement could not be reviewed, even while he was reviewing it.

Augustine then entered the argument once again, with a letter to Sixtus of Rome. He said that everyone deserved to be damned, so if God damned some but not others then nobody had any cause for complaint. Further, the sin that is inherited is personal sin and not just a tendency to sin, and grace cannot be resisted. This last soon became the matter of controversy, and Julian of Eclanum in

Italy asserted that grace was necessary for all good works, but 'it will not follow' those who resist it. Had he stopped there he might have been known today as St Julian, but he denied original sin and was banished. Significantly, he went to Theodore of Mopsuestia, the father or grandfather of Nestorianism, which is related to Pelagianism since both are at the optimistic end of the spectrum where human nature is concerned.

The next person to be engaged in this controversy, of which the sea-travel was now over, and galley-slaves toiling in other causes, was an abbot named Valentine. He and his monks had been reading Augustine's Letter to Sixtus in the monastery refectory, and in 427 they asked Augustine to explain it. He did this so strongly that Valentine very properly responded, 'If this is so, we should not be blamed when we do wrong – it is not my fault if, according to Augustine, I have no freedom.'

However, the centre of the argument had now switched from Rome, Palestine, Sicily, Carthage, and Hippo, to the south of France where a half-way heresy called Semi-Pelagianism came into being. The Semi-Pelagians argued that there was an initial act of faith, thereby guaranteeing human free will. This act of faith would lead to an act of grace from God, which is necesary for any good work. They thus safeguarded the sovereignty of God, or they thought they did. But it was pointed out that the Semi-Pelagians, for all their attempts to be even-handed, had left human beings with the ability to set the whole process in motion. In other words, they saved themselves by their act of faith. This naturally brought objections from Augustine, but Augustine also advised his followers to be careful in preaching such a mystery as the supremacy of God, and they should always preach as if everyone present was predestined to be saved. This virtually made predestination a purely theological and theoretical matter without practical consequences. If his opponents argued that at least one person must be without sin, and even Augustine would admit that in some sense the Blessed Virgin Mary was without sin, Augustine was really forced to find that at least one person was predestined by God to damnation, though he never stated it quite like that.

Augustine died in 430 but his argument was continued by Prosper of Aquitaine; it is believed that at about the same time Pelagius, whom Augustine would never consider his enemy, died in Egypt while writing a commentary on the love of God in the Song of Songs. By an odd quirk of fate Pelagius' biblical writings survived since they were wrongly believed to have been written by Jerome; this might have amused Pelagius but would not have amused Jerome. But from this point the controversy ceased to dominate Christian thinking, though it rumbled on for another century as a distant noise in the background.

The solution, so far as there could be a solution, came in the year 529 when fourteen bishops headed by Caesarius of Arles gathered to consecrate a cathedral in the town of Orange, a name subsequently given to both a royal house and a citrus fruit. Caesarius had carefully prepared the ground and sounded out Rome and other centres, and he knew that the proposed compromise would be more widely acceptable if tried out at Orange. When the cathedral was consecrated the fourteen accepted twenty-five of Augustine's statements on grace, but not his predestination. They carefully avoided saying that grace was irresistible, but they condemned the Semi-Pelagian claim that grace came only after faith. Instead they produced a rather clumsy but workable image of faith and of grace. There is a grace which comes before faith, and is 'prevenient', the word meaning 'coming before'. Then comes faith, which is an exercise of the human will. Then, in response to that act of faith, comes 'following' grace by which, and only by which, we are enabled to do good works. Students will insist that the result of this synod is a 'faithburger', but if that is what it is, it has endured to our day. The cathedral, unfortunately, has not. It was ruined first by barbarians and then by restorers.

The controversies over the Trinity and the Person of Christ have left us the creeds. The controversy over grace has a different memorial in the collects, which are the prayers, changing each Sunday, which precede the readings from scripture at the eucharist. Most of those which are used in the summer months are a denial of Pelagianism. There is one which, in the version of the old Book of Common Prayer, begins, 'Lord, we pray thee that thy grace may always prevent and follow us, and make us continually to be given to all good works ...', which has led many hearers to think about God's grace preventing us doing what we should not, but is really a reference to prevenient and following grace. But since the 1960s the cold wind of modern translation has whipped this collect into odd shapes. The new Roman mass has produced something rather attractive: 'Go before us in our pilgrimage of life, anticipate our needs and prevent our falling ...', which brings to mind the page-boy following King Wenceslas through the snow, and has not the remotest connection with the original message.

It would be nice to think that the whole church sat back after the decisions of Orange in 529 and worried about this no longer. In fact they have never ceased worrying. In every generation there seems to be someone who is so concerned to assert the full majesty and power of God that any free will must be denied. Such was Thomas Bradwardine in the Middle Ages, and such was John Calvin in the Reformation era. The entire seventeenth century sometimes seems to have been a large-scale re-play of the Pelagian controversy, with Jansenism representing the Augustinian cause within Roman Catholicism.

In the nineteenth century a rather mild form of Semi-Pelagianism, or Quarter-Pelagianism, made itself felt. In theological terms its most daring venture was the doctrine of total sanctification, or the ability of at least a few Christians to live without sin. This doctrine had been set forth by John Wesley as part of his lifelong crusade against Calvinism. It had declined amongst Methodists until revived towards the end of the last century in the Holiness movement, which largely led into Pentecostalism. Amongst Roman Catholics the equivalent was the doctrine of the Immaculate Conception of the Blessed Virgin Mary, which stressed that at least one human being could be without sin. This might be linked with the devotion to the Sacred Heart, or the humanity of Christ, in a period when humanity rather than divinity was uppermost in the Christian mind. It may be that the twentieth century has seen something of a swing away from this extreme, though it would be rash to predict that Augustine or Calvin or Jansen were on the way back.

Yet there can be few Christians who have not been troubled, at least momentarily, by the paradox of human responsibility and God's almighty power. Ultimately it is a paradox, with no solution, and the 'faithburger' of Orange is just another junk-food answer to keep us going until we can find something more nutritious. People shrug their shoulders and say it is all in the stars or somebody up there does not like them or 'That's life, i'nt it?' Other people say it all depends on what you make of it and nobody will do it for you. Neither outlook can be correct, and neither outlook can satisfy, but they may be starting points.

Until the rise of modern electronic navigation it was the custom for ships' compasses to have large balls of iron on either side, so that the compass would not be deflected by minor bits of metal. Perhaps the thing to do with Pelagius and Augustine is to tie one to one side and the other to the other, and steer safely in between.

12

Augustine

'There was a pear-tree near our vineyard, heavy with fruit, but fruit that was not very attractive to see or to taste. A gang of young rowdies, including myself, went out late one night to bring down the pears and take them away. We scarcely tasted them before throwing them to the pigs.' This is sin, and if Augustine had a highly developed sense of sin, it was this pointless and petty sin rather than anything more glamourous.

He was born in what is now Algeria, in 352, the son of a Christian mother, Monica, and an unbelieving father. The territory was rich and fertile, but somewhat in the shadow of more advanced provinces. African Christians were inclined to go to extremes, to lay great stress on religious experience, and to regard Christ not so much as a saviour who had suffered as the wisdom made available to human beings. This was seen in the Bible which was all-important; the bishop's high place in the church was due to his being the interpreter of the scriptures. And there were even Christians who made it a point of honour to read nothing but the Bible, though few had anything to read except the Bible anyway, and to speak in that curious Latin in which the old Bible was read. For Roman Africa was a Latin-speaking colony, perhaps more Latin-speaking even than Italy, and Augustine never learned Greek. Yet Latin faded away as one left the coast, to be replaced by Punic. And Christianity faded also; upland peoples were more responsive to demons, who were held to rule this world as God ruled the next. But if intensity was high, commitment was low. Augustine's flock in later days tended to be grasping and self-indulgent.

As an expensively educated youth, Augustine joined the Manichaeans. These latter-day Gnostics held that the creation was alive, and light from heaven was imprisoned by eating, but the elect would release that light when they ate it. As Augustine later wrote, he was 'bearing food to those who were called elect and holy, that in the factory of their own stomachs they should turn it into angels and deities by whom I was to be set free'. The Manicheans did believe in a suffering Christ, but one crucified throughout the whole universe, which was later denied by Augustine, writing: 'From one particular region of the earth in which alone the true God was worshipped and where alone such a man could be born, chosen men were sent throughout the whole world.' Again, the Manichaean faith was closely tied to specific scientific beliefs, as Christianity was not, and when Augustine realized that those scientific revelations were false his faith began to crack. But anyone wishing to understand the Manichaeans has only to read the New Age writings of our own day.

By that time Augustine had left Africa. Bidding farewell to a weeping Monica he set sail for Rome to pursue his studies. Then to Milan, where he became a teacher of rhetoric, or public speaking. Followed by Monica, he agreed to a marriage with one of his own class, which meant putting aside the woman with whom he had lived for many years, and who had borne him a son, of whom he was to write, 'His great intelligence filled me with a kind of wonder ...' He then came under the influence of the bishop, Ambrose, who convinced Augustine that God was not of the material world, and neither was the soul. Yet the theology of Ambrose would never have satisfied Augustine, for Ambrose believed that philosophy was not helpful to Christianity but a rival faith. All that was necessary was to study the scriptures and take the difficult Old Testament parts in symbolic ways.

His conversion was gradual; in fact it was preceded by a vision or religious experience which was based on the philosophy of Plato. That philosophy led him on, as he was to write in his *Confessions*: 'Now that I had read the books of the Platonists and had been set by them towards the search for a truth that is not material, I came to see your invisible things which are known through the things that are made.' Yet he did not think of Plato's philosophy as more than a pointer to something else. 'It is one thing to see the land of peace from a wooded mountaintop, yet not find the way to it and struggle hopelessly far from the way …' Augustine did find the way. Overcome by a sense of crisis, he had left a friend and stepped into a garden. 'And suddenly I heard a voice from some nearby home, a boy's voice or a girl's voice, I do not know …,' and it said, 'Take and read,' and Augustine went back inside, took the Bible, and read Romans 13.13, which he applied to his own life of selfishness, and, 'Then we went in to my mother and told her, to her great joy.' His early years of ambition and self-indulgence, though not unusual, weighed heavily on him, and he accused himself of having been slow to answer the call of God. 'Late have I loved you, O beauty, so old and so new.'

There followed a period of retreat with friends in the foothills of the Alps, after which they returned to Africa. His career in rhetoric was out of the question, and so was marriage. In his birthplace he established something of a monastic community, the first in that province, though it was more distinguished for learning than for privations. And around Augustine were already gathered those friends and followers who were to give the North African church so many learned bishops – perhaps out of place in such an unlearned land. But Augustine's son was not to be amongst them – he was baptised with his father, but died in his youth.

We know so much intimate detail of Augustine's life through his *Confessions*, written about 400 when he was already Bishop of Hippo. They are not confessions in the modern sense, but a confession of faith; the main part is autobiography but there is then a section on memory, one on time, and another on Genesis. The work, taken down by the stenographers who flourished in that age, was copied and read throughout the known world, and made Augustine famous. It has been described as a personal account of the whole story of the world, which accounts for the section on Genesis, and also as an attempt to find himself. It could have been both. It provides his teaching in its most attractive form, as when he writes of the will as depending on a capacity for delight. In fact delight is at the heart of Augustine's thinking, though there is also a tendency to see mathematics as the most certain of the sciences, and in some sense the most religious, and there is a deep interest in music as a way to understand human nature.

He described the memory as a tomb in which lay the soul, as Lazarus did in his grave. Augustine never lost this deep sense of the past, and he wrote, addressing himself to God, 'Great is the power of memory ... how shall I find you if I am without memory of you?', and 'In recalling you to mind I have advanced beyond those parts of memory which I have in common with animals ...' His idea of memory was linked to his ideas of development: 'We look upon the heavens and the earth, and they cry aloud that they were made. For they change and vary ...' While God does not. In his study of Genesis, Augustine was faced with the problem of what God did before making his creation, which assumed that God was bound by time and did not bind it. 'How could countless ages pass when you, the author and creator of all ages, had not made them?' At the end of a lengthy discussion of time he ruefully admitted, 'I still do not know what time is.'

But there was always a danger that an able Christian would be snatched by a bishop-less church, and Augustine avoided towns lacking bishops. But in 391 he visited Hippo, where the Greek-speaking bishop wanted a presbyter to preach in Latin, and a presbyter he unwillingly became. This led on to his being assistant bishop and assured successor four years later, in defiance of all the rules. Though he moved his community to Hippo, he had ended his life as a scholar withdrawn from the world. He was now in the thick of affairs, and almost the first thing that concerned him was Donatism.

Hippo was largely a pagan city, and most of its Christians were Donatists. During Augustine's lifetime both pagans and Donatists dwindled away, but the Donatists, who had at one time threatened the very existence of Augustine's church, decreased under state repression. Augustine tried persuasion without result, and he may have widened the gap between the two factions when he and the Bishop of Carthage moved to abolish the rowdy feasts for the martyrs which had long been a popular feature of the North African church. Again, Augustine was very much the bishop of a coastal city relying on his co-religionists amongst the landowners to protect clergy upcountry from Donatist pressures and violence; he himself seldom ventured into the interior.

But in 411 there was a state investigation, to which the Donatists proceeded in force, and this was disastrous for the Donatist cause. They preached freedom of religion in an age when such a thing was unknown, and they themselves had never granted it to others, and had also been the first to demand state mediation between themselves and their opponents. Augustine carefully avoided the question of the church and its nature, and concentrated on the history of the schism, on which the Donatist case was weak – particularly as the Donatists had persecuted those who had seceded from their own ranks. The result was that most Donatists in the cities abandoned their church; Augustine found many devout and sincere Christians swelling his ranks. But in the countryside the Donatists could and did continue, though some, unable to compromise or to resist, resorted to suicide. Augustine approved of this policy, and his growing rigidity on grace rather than free will may have meant that he took freedom of conscience more lightly, and saw the grace of God determining everything. But without Augustine the result would have been the same; the state could not tolerate violence and disorder, and Constantine saw church and empire as different aspects of the same thing.

As bishop, Augustine spent most mornings judging property cases; the civil courts were tardy and costly and many Christians prefered arbitration. It showed human nature at its most grasping, and Augustine loathed it. But if those he met in this way were scarcely saints, there were precious few civil servants with much desire to serve, and many of the clergy were little better. Scandals were frequent. And then there was the slave trade; Augustine hated that most of all. But he excelled as a preacher, and for nearly forty years he would put himself in the place of his hearers and then carry them out of their world into his, taking some mystery of the Bible and making it plain. And in everything he leaned on Plato.

In Plato there is a distinction between the shadow we see and the reality we do not see, and Augustine was not the first Christian to describe our life as the shadow and God as the real thing. 'My imaginary Rome is not the real Rome, nor am I really there ...' wrote Augustine, to show that there can be grades of reality, and yet Plato was not his religion. In his view Plato only began what Christ was to complete, and the only true philosophy was that of Christ. Thus even words were not sure guides; had Augustine seen the painting by the Belgian artist Magritte of a tobacco pipe over the words, 'This is not a pipe,' he would have agreed. Symbols are good, but they are only symbols. Yet some aspects of Plato's thought were rejected; Augustine could not accept creation from something which existed before, and he saw in creation a continuing development from its beginnings.

Yet the greatest conflict was to come over Pelagianism. And, as Peter Brown has put it, 'The Pelagian man was essentially a separate individual; the man of Augustine is always about to be engulfed in vast, mysterious, solidarities.' If Augustine is said to have discovered the subconscious, it is because he viewed humanity as all one lump, from which individuals were saved by the grace of God. And just as he saw the individual as bound by the nature of the group, so Augustine saw that individual as influenced and determined by childhood experience. The pear tree was always there, and the emphasis on memory seen in the *Confessions* never left him. On this question Pelagius and his disciples were followers of the older views of classical antiquity; Augustine was the first thinker of the Middle Ages. Yet Augustine was no dualist, seeing good and evil as equals. Of evil he wrote: 'It is nothing but the corruption of natural measure, form, and order. What is called an evil nature is a corrupt nature. If it were not corrupt it would be good. but even when it is corrupted, so far as it remains a natural thing, it is good.' And his violence against the Pelagians, leading to active intervention by the state, was in defence of something positive. As he said of them, '... the Pelagians are a new brand of heretics who assert the freedom of

the will in such a way as to leave no room for the Grace of God.'
Finally, Augustine was writing, and Pelagius was agonizing, in
what Gerald Bonner has called 'an age of active cruelty, passive
selfishness, and unbridled lust and avarice'. An age in which the
public remedy for all this was to make punishments even more
brutal than they had been before. If neither Pelagius nor Augustine kept a balanced view, they had good cause to be extremists.

But Augustine is normally regarded as obsessed with sin and
obsessed with sex. And, like everyone else, his biology was bad.
He believed that before the Fall sex would have been used 'as need
required, the generating organs being moved by the will, and not
by lust', and he went to some lengths to prove this. And he did
believe that gender applied to the soul; there was an Eve side,
which was active, and an Adam side, which was mental and
contemplative, and which should be encouraged. But he did not
go so far as to say that all would be male in heaven. And if he
expected the clergy of his church not to live with their wives,
which is quite a different thing from clergy never having had
wives, this was hardly his own invention. The same thing had
been suggested at the Council of Nicaea, though it was not taken
further at that time. Altogether, Augustine's view of sexuality is
described by Bonner as 'a remarkably sane one', but remarkable
just because of his theory being what it was, and the times being
what they were.

Yet what is even more remarkable is that Augustine never
reached a decision on that Spaghetti Junction, that Grand Central
Station, that ultimate crossroads of the early church, the origin of
the soul. Whether it came from the parents, or one parent, or was
individually created by God, he never decided, though he thought
about it, presumably only off and on, for four years. He toyed in
early years with the idea of a single 'world-soul', but then moved
to individual souls; his view of people as parts of a mass did not
go all the way. There is a grand if gruesome tale from his days in
Alpine retreat when 'the boys had found a centipede, and the
whole company gathered round to watch the way in which its
chopped up portions continued to move of their own accord',
causing him to ask, 'Is the animating soul of the beast also

divisible?' If it were, then parents could divide their souls to provide for their offspring. That he did not go further on this subject is all the more remarkable since it lay at the heart of the Pelagian controversy; Caelestius, the friend and disciple of Pelagius, held that children's souls were all brand new and thus could not be tainted with original sin. Augustine might have brandished the dismembered centipede in reply, but did not.

Some few years past a lieutenant-colonel of Ethiopian army engineers, writing from Egypt where he had sought refuge from Mengistite tyranny, wrote to the physics departments of Scottish universities telling them how they might solve the problem of the origin of the soul. It involved using electronic instruments of a certain frequency at the moment of conception. The physicists decided, after some soul-searching but no searching for souls, to turn the whole problem over to the theologians, who still have it. We may feel the lieutenant-colonel's answer to the problem was a trifle mechanical, but his identificaation of the problem deserved praise.

Of course modern Christians find it odd that early Christians should ever have been concerned about the origin of the soul. It seems bizarre and unimportant. And yet it is a very modern concern, under another name. At the present time the whole world seems to be divided into angry crowds demonstrating for or against abortion. The issue is whether the foetus is human from the time of conception, or later, or not until birth, which is another way of asking when it has a soul, which asks how the soul is given to the body.

In 410 barbarians sacked the city of Rome, leading many to ask if this was not a punishment for deserting the old Roman gods. Augustine's answer, hammered out over thirteen years of effort, was *The City of God*, in which he drew a very Platonic distinction between the city of this world and that of the next. He was the more able to do this because the Roman empire had always been oppressive and the Christian Roman empire of his own day was thoroughly corrupt, but he treated paganism as a matter of history. Pagans had come to admit that their own faith was becoming a relic of a glorious past, so it made sense to dig up that past and present it in all its bloodthirsty greediness. But Augustine's comments of the sufferings of the citizens of Rome cannot but appal the reader. He tells Roman pagans they should be glad that the Christian barbarians would not attack churches, so that the pagans might shelter there. Of those tortured to give up wealth which was not eternal, even if they had none, he suggests that they 'had perhaps some craving for wealth', and of those put to death in 'cruel ways', 'no one has ever died who was not destined to die some time'. As for the women who were raped, 'nothing that another person does with the body ... is any fault of the person who suffers it ...'

But the next set of barbarians were the Vandals, and they crossed into North Africa eighty thousand strong. Since only about twelve thousand can have been active fighters, any sort of resistance could have stopped them dead, but revolts and intrigues had worn out the state and its army, and the Vandals conquered and tortured at will. Augustine died, in the year 430, while they were at the gates, and the city filled with refugees. And the once fertile lands of North Africa became deserts, and deserts they are still. It might seem that Augustine could have done something to prevent this horror by teaching duty in government, but no single person can do everything. History is full of examples of small groups of desperate men overthrowing vast civilizations; our hold on life is weak at best, and that Augustine knew. It was what he taught against the Donatists who believed in a perfect church, and the Pelagians who believed in the capacity of human beings to do good, and anyone else who had forgotten the pear trees of their youth.

13

Celtic Church

That the Celts had 'more developed organs of respiration', while the Saxons had 'a larger volume of intestines', was something which so impressed the Victorian poet Matthew Arnold that, he said, it 'sets one spirits in a glow'. It readily explained why the French were voluble, and the Germans always belching.

We are not quite so anatomical in our ideas of race today, but something of the distinction lingers. The Celts are thought to be a race, and to be soulful and gentle, while the Saxons are coarse and materialistic. If you are a Celt then you can pray and be sensitive to the environment but if you are a Saxon then you can only belch. Indeed, much of the world's troubles can be blamed on the Saxons; they set up the market economy and they wrecked the ozone layer. And on the religious side, it was the aggressive and insensitive Saxon tradition of Christianity which predominated, and we must now restore the gentle Celtic tradition in order to have a balanced and true Christianity.

Nora Chadwick, in her book *The Celts*, puts the conventional view very clearly. 'With the Teutonic world which succeeds it (the Celtic world) we enter an ordered domain, where cause and effect follow one another with mathematical certainty and precision, where events follow one another in logical sequence, where the established time sequence can be relied on, where an established geography limits human journeys, where men and animals behave according to prescribed laws. In the earlier Celtic order all these conditions resolve themselves and are recreated by the imagination, not always by fixed laws, but by the tradition of a poet's theme or his will to reshape his subject. Memory is flexible, the spoken word more fluid than history. All this was inevitably changed with the introduction of writing.' This is all very well until you think about it, but the whole point of this so-called Celtic religion is that you do not have to think about it. Logical sequence does not exist. There is no thought – just imagination.

There is more to it than this. People who are thought to be Celtic, whether Irish or Scottish Highlander or Welsh or Breton, are more likely to be included in folk groups than those who are thought to be Saxon. But they are less likely to be included in accountancy training courses. Because of a false distinction between different peoples, who in fact are very much the same people, discrimination is practised throughout the English-speaking world. And to show that this distinction is false, we must ask if there was a Celtic people, or a Celtic church.

The answer is yes and no, which is the answer to all serious questions. There was a church amongst Celtic-speaking peoples, but whether it was different enough to be called a Celtic church is doubtful. Yet it has served many to believe that it was very different indeed. It has served Scots who wanted to support their difference from the English. It has served Irish who wanted to support their difference from everybody. Indeed, anyone in Ireland who does not fit the Celtic stereotype is assumed to be descended from a survivor of the Spanish Armada. It has served the English who want to establish their difference from the Scots and the Irish and the Welsh. It has served Protestants who needed a Protestant history from before the Reformation, and could create a non-Roman Bible-reading Presbyterianism of the Celts. It has served Roman Catholics who wanted to show how well they would have done had they not fallen under Protestant and Anglo-Saxon rule. It has served anyone who wanted a golden age. It now serves Christians accused of polluting the planet, and who can argue that Celtic Christianity was environmentally friendly and did not involve heavy industry or chemicals on the land. (Few people of any religion had much heavy industry or chemical fertiliser in ancient times.) And the idea of the Celtic church also serves those who rely on the cosmic forces of nature which emerge at certain places and feed the psyche. The idea can be adapted for any purpose at all.

But who were the Celts? There is a good deal of doubt. Some say they were an actual race, some a military alliance. The latest book says that there were no Celts, no Gauls, no Asterix. It was all a misunderstanding, and presumably the peoples of North Western Europe did not derive their culture from Central Europe or Asia or anywhere else, but made it up on the spot. Some of it perhaps very recently. Of course this view will horrify those who believe that the Irish and Scots and Welsh and Bretons could never have created a culture. They must have bought it on the cheap or found it washed up on the beach.

But the more traditional history is that the Celtic homeland was in Asia, from which conveniently vague location they moved to Alpine valleys and there adopted a language and culture, themselves of unknown origin. They were noted for military skills, and their iron-age weapons enabled them to subdue bronze-age peoples, but it is not clear why they were eventually defeated by the Romans. To say that the Romans were disciplined but the Celts were not is not good enough. If the Celts had no discipline, how could they, beyond all other peoples, threaten the Romans?

Another thing about the Celts was their fascination with heads, usually detached from their bodies and hung around doors. This disarming habit has left certain Irish cathedral doorways bright with these objects, though carved in stone and not removed from bodies. Decapitation apart, their religion provided easy access to the supernatural, and this is hardly surprising as they had little sense of sin. There was no real need for salvation in Celtic thought, which was about as far as could be from the modern Christianity of the so-called Celtic fringe. In fact the harsh tone of Roman Catholicism and Presbyterianism in lands of Celtic culture may have arisen to counter-balance the theological easi-ness of Celtic thought. But there was also a rich imagery on which Christianity could build. There were tales of rebirth, and lands of perpetual youth and summer. Curiously for those in northern lands, and perhaps suggesting origins in southern lands, their calendar was not based on the sun but on the internal cycles of cattle and sheep, though these did depend on the sun as could be seen when they were moved to Australia.

The Celts managed to hack and slash their way across a good deal of the known world. Of course the word 'Gaul' means a Celt, and there are a number of countries named for this. Wales is one of them; in French it is 'Pays de Galles', and its Welsh name, Cymri, is also found in Cumbria and in the Cumbrae Islands in the Clyde. Then there is Galway in Ireland, and Galloway in south-west Scotland, and Argyle in Scotland which is Galloway wrong way round. There are three areas named Galicia – one in the Ukraine, one in Asia Minor (Galatia, where Paul sent his epistle), and one in Spain, which could make the Armada sailors more Celtic than the Irish. But none of these peoples are descended from Celts; they are descended from peoples who were conquered by Celtic overlords and adopted their language and ways, willingly or otherwise. Probably unwillingly.

This having been said, there is even more doubt about the Anglo-Saxons. Nobody ever saw an Anglo-Saxon. The Angles and Saxons lived in parts of northern Europe rather distant from each other, and the claim of the English to be descended from Anglo-Saxons was as mythical as anything ever said about the Celts. But if there are no Celts and no Anglo-Saxons then we are tempted to conclude there are no human beings at all in Britain, which the French have long suspected. In fact the legend of the Anglo-Saxons is fairly recent; in the Middle Ages there was a happy theory that the English were refugees from ancient Troy, and 'You are a Trojan' was a way of saying someone was truly English. To this people Christianity was brought by Joseph of Arimathaea, who settled at Glastonbury, and thus England could claim apostolic foundations. It was in the sixteenth century that a German ancestry became fashionable, and in the seventeenth century the parliamentarian party re-wrote Saxon history to make it favour democracy, and then re-wrote Magna Carta to make that democratic as well.

To make this convincing it had to be argued that the Anglo-Saxons exterminated the Britons or pushed them out to the north and the west. This was easily done, and the theory of Saxon dominance was taken up by later writers of whom the most colourful, if not the most scholarly, was the Edinburgh anatomist Robert Knox, who is more famed for hiring men to procure him subjects for his art, those same men having, in a slack market, aroused widespread disfavour by diversifying into manufacture. Yet the main drift of the Anglo-Saxon argument was that such people were natural democrats and thus natural Protestants. On the other hand, Celts were imaginative but unable to cope with logical sequence, and so needed priests to think for them, which made them natural Catholics. All sorts of terrible things were sure to happen if the natural Catholics were allowed a major voice in government, or if Catholicism spread to those who were natural Protestants, and there was then nobody left to do the thinking. The relics of such views still influence England's view of Ireland, and lead to distrust of continental Europe and the transference of sovereignty to Brussels.

Yet it is very hard to disentangle the Celts (who are not Celts) from the Anglo-Saxons (who are not Anglo-Saxons). To begin with the idea that the Saxons replaced the Britons, they may have replaced the overlords, and they may have taken some of the land, much as the Celts did before them, but they did not replace the bulk of the population, and they did not take all of the land. They lived with the Britons, and they eventually intermarried with them. The process is shown by the study of place names, and by blood-groups. The names of places throughout England, as well as lowland Scotland, show patches of old Celtic names mixed with patches of Saxon names. Combinations such as 'Eaglesfield', where the 'eagle' or 'ecclesia' is the old British for church, and the 'field' is Saxon for field, suggest that the Saxons knew and recognized British churches, and were probably influenced by and to some extent Christianized by them. Well before Augustine reached Canterbury in 597, and met British bishops, the mission to the Saxons could well have been under way.

As for blood groups, there is a higher proportion of group A amongst Angles and Saxons and Jutes, and a higher proportion of group O amongst ancient Britons. As a result, statistics from blood donors will show the ancestry of present-day inhabitants in different areas. In fact they do show that there is a higher proportion of group O in northern England than in southern, but the difference is slight, even for rural areas where there have been hardly any incomers. The eastern half of Ireland is much like England in racial origin, while the western half has higher proportions of group O. What this tells us is that there is a general admixture of the two racial groups, unless there is some genetic factor in one racial group or the other which causes them to give or not give blood. But the outcome of all this study is the almost universal agreement that the English are of mainly British descent, with a lesser Saxon element in their ancestry. But whether this makes them Celtic is another matter; that word has been so misused that we may sympathize with the academic who said he couldn't see why he should switch to Celtic when there was nothing the matter with Fahrenheit.

But having dealt with the Celts we must now deal with their church. There is no doubt that the British and Irish churches followed older customs from Gaul, commonly called 'Gallican', which had died out on the mainland. But these customs were scarcely all that vital. The British and Irish churches were still a part of the Western church, introduced in the days of the Roman empire, and using Latin in their worship. For, despite personal devotions in the common tongue, Christianity meant using Latin.

This may strike the modern reader as extraordinary. We have heard so much about the enormity of making Highland Scots or Western Irish speak English in the last century that we tend to assume they can only function in a Celtic tongue. They would suffer psychological torments and malfunctions if required to function in anything else. Yet there is a dark side to this notion; it is rooted in the idea that Celtic peoples are less well-adapted than others and cannot change. Yet anyone can learn languages, and most people in the world are aware of more than one, and use more than one. It used to be Italian for opera and German for science and French for cooking and English for sanitary fixtures and football and the long weekend, so why not Latin for religion? Furthermore, Celtic tongues were not written, and if you wanted to read or to write you needed Latin. Some Celtic speakers did have a form of writing called 'ogham' which may have had Roman origins; it was a system of slashes not unlike modern computer language, but it only worked on stone or wood which was a bit on the slow side.

Christianity in Roman times was centred in the south-east and in the north-west of England. By 450 there were separate dioceses and separate bishops for Carlisle and Galloway in south-west Scotland. A century later there were also bishops on the Clyde, the Forth, and the Tweed. Ninian may have gone as bishop to Whithorn in Galloway as early as 400, but to a church which had existed for some time. There is no evidence of his having been a missionary, though his name has been connected with many other places in Scotland. This was partly because Galloway was clearly under York until quite late on in the Middle Ages, so that when it was joined to other Scottish bishoprics a Scottish history had to be invented for it by making Ninian Scottish. But in the 1920s, when Irishness was unpopular amongst some Scots, and Columba's Irish origins made him unwelcome, there was an attempt to prove that Ninian evangelized north-east Scotland. This was done by arguing that wherever a church in Celtic times was dedicated to a saint it was because it was founded by that saint. Thus you could prove that Ninian travelled to certain places and founded certain churches, and you could then prove that if a church was dedicated to Ninian it was founded by Ninian since you only found churches dedicated to Ninian where he had travelled. The argument was circular.

As for Columba, who arrived in Iona in the year 563 and founded a monastery, the evidence for his life is early, but that he was a missionary is unlikely. That was not his work; it was what a later generation thought should have been his work. Patrick was obviously earlier and here it seems that Palladius was sent as bishop to already existing churches in Ireland in the fifth century, and was followed by Patrick. Yet earlier evidence of Irish Christianity suggests it had already begun in the south, and that Patrick was a later bishop only working in the north. Christianity, just as it moved north of the limits of Roman territory in Britain, almost certainly moved across to Ireland long before the Roman withdrawal early in the fifth century. Christianity in Britain and Ireland did not wait for the heroic founders of legend; we know that in the year 314 four British bishops went to a council at Arles in France, and it has even been argued that in 79 there were two people in York who must have met Paul the Apostle. And that was long before Columba or Ninian or Patrick.

Moving to north-east Scotland, in the early sixteenth century a Martyrology and a Breviary were compiled in Aberdeen in order to show that the Scottish church had always been distinct from that of England, and that the church of Andrew of Scotland was older than that of Peter of York. Since Andrew brought his brother Peter to Christ, it has long been customary to use foundation by Andrew to offset the claims of Peter, whether Peter of Rome or Peter of York. Thus Constantinople claimed foundation by Andrew, and Russia claimed evangelization by Andrew, and the Russian navy used the flag of St Andrew, while the Scots made much of having the bones of Andrew in Scotland, though they were also in Greece. But the Aberdeen effort took all kinds of ancient Scots worthies and wove their legends into one narrative accounting for Scots church history without any English, and incidentally causing them all to visit Gregory the Great in Rome, though he was not yet born. This last established that Scotland was directly under Rome and not under York. Disentangling the stories that went into the Aberdeen machinery from those that went out is a perilous work, and at the end of it the stories are only the product of an earlier machinery, and an earlier machinery than that. But that is how history must be studied.

Yet we are left with the words of Nora Chadwick about the two worlds; in the one cause and effect follow one another with mathematical certainty and precision, and in the other all traditions resolve one another and are recreated by the imagination. The reader is not so much reminded of historical differences between civilizations, as of differences between modern

104

philosophers and modern scientists. Nora Chadwick's words were written at the end of the 1960s, in which a philosophical fire-storm had raged, and this was largely directed at order and artificiality and the art of writing which Dr Chadwick held to have swept away the old Celtic order. But they also recall the famous statement of Albert Einstein, 'God does not play dice,' which might be re-phrased as 'God is a God of order and is not a Celt', while the equally famous rejoinder of Neils Bohr, 'Who are you to tell God what to do?' might be re-phrased as 'God can be as Celtic as he wishes.' Our view of reality will inevitably colour our view of Celtic history.

Then there is the other main characteristic of Celtic religion carried over into Christianity, which is the closeness of the natural to the supernatural. This closeness is supposed to be expressed in the design of Celtic crosses, in which a circle joins the arms of the cross, and may represent eternity or creation; on the other hand, it may have originated in order to prevent the arms from falling off. Such closeness may be part of the Christian faith, but it is only part, and in the long run it must be balanced with a recognition that God is awe-inspiring and distant, and that if he were not awe-inspiring and distant there would be no miracle in God taking human nature. Again, the Celtic closeness of the natural and the supernatural assumes that human beings are as nearly faultless as makes no difference, and nobody who has lived in this world can believe that for very long. On its own, Celtic spirituality is inadequate, though in combination with opposites it can be very enriching indeed.

But enthusiasm for Celtic spirituality is sometimes linked with a particular interpretation of early church history. In the preface to a collection of Celtic Christian prayers and poems, actually compiled in the Scottish Highlands in the last century but assumed to have come down from Celtic antiquity a thousand years before, Esther de Waal has argued that 'The foundation stone of such an outlook is simply that this is God's world, that creation is good, and that material things reflect their creator. Perhaps because they were converted to Christianity very early the Irish received the Gospel at a time when the church was sure that the goodness of God healed and restored the whole of creation.' This may be God's world, but it is not obviously good in every respect, and to suggest that the early church was sure that the goodness of God healed and restored the whole of creation implies that there was a later change, though at least Esther de Waal does not blame this on Augustine. The goodness of God heals and restores, but this is not a finished work, and there is still much to be done.

In a world in which kinship with nature is strong, and it had better be strong if we are to survive without drowning in our own garbage, it is not only natural but perhaps necessary that Christianity should seek devotions and outlooks which link the faith and the environment. The Celtic treasury of prayers and of poems has that characteristic, though in this it is not alone. In a world in which philosophy seems to disregard order in favour of spontaneity, it is equally natural that Christianity should seek an ancient form in which spontaneity seemed to be paramount, though it is doubtful if this was actually the case. But there are two dangers in this. The first is that the re-structuring of Christianity may hardly occur before the tide has changed and Roman regularity is once again the norm. The second is that giving Celtic names to a type of prayers implies that certain peoples have certain characteristics, and restricts their freedom to act except in certain pre-determined ways. If we cannot avoid the cruder manifestations of racism between so-called Celt and so-called Anglo-Saxon, there is not much hope of our understanding and appreciating French, Germans, Russians, Africans, Gypsies, Chinese, or – for some the hardest task of all – Australians.

Having begun with one English poet it is proper to end with another, and so be finished with the entire tribe of them. Wordsworth heard of someone who claimed to have heard a young woman singing as she reaped in the Highlands. This he made into a poem: 'Will no one tell me what she sings? Perhaps the plaintive numbers flow, For old, unhappy, far-off things, And battles long ago : Or is it some more humble lay, Familiar matter of today? Some natural sorrow, loss, or pain, That has been and may be again?' There is all too much tendency to give the Celtic speakers credit for singing of unhappy far-off things, and to forget that they are just as concerned as anyone else with familiar matters of today and natural sorrow or loss or pain. In short, they are people.

14

Women

During the 1960s, when almost anything went, a Swedish legis-
lator proposed that the Welfare State should provide all citizens
with sexual satisfaction. Nothing further was heard on this
subject, but it was one aspect of an outlook which is still very
much with us. Everyone can expect to be sexually satisfied,
whatever their state, and whatever the cost to others. And to deny
this is to be part of a Calvinist, Augustinian, culture, put about by
the church in order to keep people's minds on their work and so
please their employers. Before Augustine it was all very much like
Margaret Mead's *Coming of Age in Samoa* and there were no
sexual restrictions at all, and women were not thought to be
inferior. The church changed all that. And the church is still asked
if it is ever going to stop interfering in the natural order of things.
And it is assumed that lack of rule in this field will benefit women.
If women are physically weaker than men, it would seem natural
that the law should protect them, but it is taken for granted that
total free enterprise in the sexual sphere will guarantee the rights
of women. Total free enterprise never guarantees anything. That
is the point of it.

In fact the church had to work, and still has to work, with the
common cultural background of its day. And this was not quite
the Samoa of Margaret Mead, assuming that even Samoa was the
Samoa of Margaret Mead. If the church had any effect on the
sexual ethics of its day, this effect was limited. It is limited today.
To suppose that there was a time when Christian ethics could
radically change sexual customs and the status of women in

society is unrealistic. The church tried with varying degrees of success in varying situations, but was as much influenced by society as it influenced society.

So the first question we must ask is what the world of antiquity thought about women. The answer is, not very much. On the one hand, some followed Aristotle in believing that women were essentially males who had gone wrong before birth, while others held that they were a sub-species of human being who were intended to exist, rather than an unfortunate accident. There was also a view that the uterus was the dominant organ in a woman, which led to 'hysteria', which word is derived from the name for uterus, and that the uterus made women more animal than human. Mixed with these views were others which derived from the same ignorance of human physiology. Some believed with Aristotle that everything inherited by the child came from the father, while the mother provided nothing but a place in which to grow. Others believed that each parent provided seed, though the father's shaped the nobler parts of the body and the mother's shaped the rest. Again, there was a widespread belief that the male body was weakened by sexual activity, and that chastity led to greater height as well as better health. On the other hand, sexual activity was essential for women whose health would otherwise run down.

There were about ten different theories of reproduction, each tied to a theory of the place of women in the scheme of things. All of these theories were seriously flawed. None of the theories agreed with any of the others. Each citizen seems to have held about three of these theories. At first, we may wonder how the human race survived, but when we think of it this is not all that diffferent from the diversity of sexual beliefs in Western life today. And, if it might have seemed that there was one biological theory which led to the inferior status of women in the Greek and Roman world, we must conclude that this was not so. It was taken for granted that women were inferior, and the various theories were attempts to explain this.

As if this were not enough, the early Christians were faced with a bewildering maze of laws about marriage, concubinage, and inheritance. The Roman empire restricted marriages between those of different social classes; if Hippolytus blamed Callistus for allowing concubinage in the Roman church it must be admitted that only thus could high-born Christian women find husbands, since there were not enough high-born men in the church to go round. Again, the empire had strict rules requiring aristocratic widows and widowers to marry within a certain time. Inheritance depended on marriage, and being unmarried was being anti-social. Yet many did not wish to be married, and when men discovered that Christian monks had discovered ways of living in celibacy they were impressed, not so much because they wanted to offer their lives to God, as because they wanted to enjoy the health they associated with chastity.

As for women, they can hardly be blamed for seeking an alternative to a marriage before puberty followed by constant pregnancies, but without the affection normally associated with marriage. Affection there sometimes was, and there was a surprising degree of affection of fathers for daughters, but not normally between husband and wife. Yet even this must be qualified; the evidence we have is almost exclusively upper class, and there may have been much more affection in other social classes. Even upper class husbands have left monuments stating how they loved their wives. But these were probably a minority; it is true that virtually all monuments to wives do say they were loved, but husbands would hardly spend money to commemorate wives to whom they were indifferent.

As for the ways in which chastity might be achieved, a limited diet was held to be the key, and obviously a diet which is totally inadequate will eliminate the sexual rhythms of a man or a woman, if they do not die of malnutrition first. For it was held by many that these sexual activities could be and should be controlled by the will, and brought into action only when it was desired to conceive a child. There is a relic of this thought in the late night hymn associated with Compline, 'Before the ending of the day ...', but those who sing it seldom think of its meaning, which is perhaps just as well. It was this same idea, 'that sex and marriage belong to the order of the fall, and they will progressively disappear', as George Tavard has put it, which caused clergy in some areas to be separated from their wives. It was to be a long time before it was recognized that marriage was 'instituted of God in the time of man's innocency', as the marriage service put it, and was not a result of the fall.

Yet despite everything that actually happened in the early church, the fundamental teaching of the New Testament is that men and women are both fully human and should be treated equally. Having said this, it may be argued that in a world in which only the male was fully human, Christ could only be fully human if he was male. Nothing else would reveal his humanity. It can also be argued that the frequent appearances of women in the gospels are only meaningful if they are regarded as the lowest of the low, to whom Christ came, and that if women are regarded as equal to men that much of the message is lost. But these problems may be left to the biblical scholars, who deserve them. There is one thing to be added; that the view of Paul as violently anti-female is not generally supported. The later epistles, which may or may not be by Paul, are against women exercising leadership in church and hardly helpful in establishing minimal rights for women. But even here there is nothing like the view of women found in pagan society. Yet having said all this, there was a wide gap between the teachings of the New Testament and the life of the early church. It is common to say that the church compromised; forced to live in a world in which women were held to be inferior, the church treated them as such. Yet the church always compromises with the world in which it finds itself, or it is isolated and ceases to exist. As has already been said, there is no such thing as pure distillate of Christianity. Whether women were more highly regarded in the church than out of it is a difficult question, but most observers seem to think that they were.

As usual, some of this was due to the Gnostics. If modern Christians are concerned about where the soul goes after death, early Christians were concerned about where it came from before birth. The Gnostics said it came from heaven, and did not fit into the body at all, so their opponents argued that it had the same shape as the body and came from the father. Tertullian said that the soul 'has ears and eyes of its own ... it has, moreover, all the other members of the body', and he went into some detail in describing how 'there are two kinds of seed – that of the body and that of the soul ...' If his aim was to refute the Gnostics his result was to put in a Christian framework the old idea that only the father contributed anything to the the child's soul.

Yet there was a confusion in the use of Gnostic language. They used 'male' and 'female' to refer to cosmic forces, not to men and women. If heavenly beings were masculine-feminine, it was also taught that this had been true of Adam until Eve, the feminine side, was cut off. Thus all women had to become men to be saved, as we have seen in the Gospel of Thomas, and yet there was a sense in which even men on earth were female until they were saved. Only the masculine-feminine whole was really male. It is in this sense that the martyr Perpetua, when she is stripped ready for death, declares that she is becoming male. Again, Irenaeus, who provided the church with its most effective defence against Gnosticism, could not help writing with something of the Gnostic vocabulary. He made the earth female and virgin, and if Eve was the first female of the Adam-Eve whole figure, then Mary is the female element of the Christ-Mary figure, and without her there is a possibility that Christ is not whole. But this would certainly take Irenaeus beyond what he intended. It still helps us to understand the significance of devotion to the Virgin Mary.

There is a relic of this argument still with us. Rosemary Radford Ruether rejects one objection to the ordination of women by saying that if a female priest cannot represent a male Christ at the altar, then a male Christ cannot have represented a female Christian on the cross, and the church should 'either ordain women or stop baptizing them'. No doubt she is right, but there are subtleties behind this apparently straightforward demand. In the ancient world only the male was seen to be a complete human being. A man could represent women, but a woman could not represent a man. Ruether's complaint only makes sense now that we know that ancient biology was wrong. The so-called 'iconic' argument against ordaining women, that a female priest cannot represent a male Christ, should be treated with respect – provided that those who use this argument can give evidence that they have really studied and accepted the nonsense of ancient biology. Possibly some of them have.

Of course there were views more ancient than those of the Gnostics. Isobel Blythe has shown that the original aim of circumcision in north-east Africa, whether of men or of women, was to surgically assert the gender of the person in question. Before circumcision, each was born in the image of the masculine-feminine deities who would otherwise be challenged if one sex or the other was not accepted. One result of this was to exaggerate the difference between male and female, and this may have lingered on. If we do not accept the views of Swedish society, in which much effort was undertaken to train up men to be nurses and women to be truck-drivers, we do have to accept that in our society the contrast between men and women has been excessive. It is possible that male-female differences having been used for opposites in theological and philosophical systems, these have then returned to plague actual men and women by placing them at opposite poles of existence. C.G. Jung the psychologist was typical of his time and place in complaining that 'woman is in the process of breaking with the purely feminine sexual pattern of unconsciousness and passivity, and has made a concession to masculine psychology by establishing herself as a visible member of society', which was 'against her psychic nature'. That the difference between male and female is rooted in the unconscious, and that there will be horrible consequences if men sing babies to sleep or women think, is part of a belief that there is nothing in life which is sexually neutral.

If we are now going to consider what the church taught about women, to a very large extent this was a by-product of the question of virginity. From what has been said of the world of antiquity, it will be seen that honest pagans were envious of male Christians' ability to live in chastity, but horrified that female Christians should attempt any such thing. As for Christian writers, they took the question of virginity very seriously . They praised it, and yet they also praised marriage. Some, such as

113

Chrysostom, were grudging about marriage without actually saying it was bad, while others such as Gregory of Nyssa, who had been married, were much more positive. On the whole virginity was considered the higher state, but it was not without its perils. There was disapproval of men such as Paul of Samosata who lived chastely with a number of women, because this led to scandal in the eyes of pagans. Yet it is not entirely clear why virginity was so praised. It was thought to be a sign of single-mindedness, and yet there must have been more to it than this. Aline Rousselle has suggested that if martyrdom was a spilling of blood, which was life, virginity was also a form of martyrdom since that blood or life was not used in sex. This may be near the heart of the matter.

There were critics of virginity, Jovinian being the best known, though his writings led Jerome to a response of such violence that he in turn had to be answered by Augustine. Unlike Gregory of Nyssa who held that there were effectively two creations, and sex came in with the second, after the fall, Augustine said that it had been there all the time. There always had been men and women, though the original Adam was both male and female. Jerome is frequently quoted as the worst woman-hater of the Christian world, but on this subject he owes much of his thought to Tertullian, and he wrote in the style normal to pagan satire. Yet he encouraged scholarship in women, and he surrounded himself with female disciples. If he was violent about the sensuality of women, he seems to have given much of his attention to women just because they were thought to have this problem. It was largely through his violent writing against women as well as his close friendships with women that he made himself unpopular in Rome and had to leave the city. He could be tender and moving about women, but also coarse and satirical. And he was some-what unrealistic; in the last two-thirds of his life he had no contact with worldly women but still went on writing furiously against them. He wrote, 'I praise marriages, I praise wedlock, but I do because they produce virgins for me. I gather roses from thorns, gold from the earth, the pearl from the shell.' But did he really believe this?

114

If the figure of Christ was seen as necessarily male, because only the male was whole, then it must be admitted that this was not developed in the early church but only in the Renaissance, when the sexuality of Christ was exalted in art and in sermons. Of this we have a solitary relic (apart from painted-over features in Renaissance paintings) in New Year's Day being the Feast of the Circumcision. But on the whole it has been customary for Christians to avoid making too much of the maleness of Christ. It is only with the recent attempt to understand the whole question of gender that it has come into the open.

On the subject of ordaining women, we have noted the theory that only a male priest can represent a male Christ. This has been reinforced by the biblical image of Christ as the bridegroom and the church as the bride though, as Ruth Edwards has written, 'The problems involved in applying the masculine image of a bridgroom to a woman priest are no greater than those of applying the feminine image of the church' to male Christians. Again, it may be thought that if women cannot be represented by Christ on the cross they can be saved through husbands who *can* be so represented. This she rejects as it 'violates the central New Testament affirmation that Christ alone mediates the New Covenant'.

But that is not really where the fault lines on this issue lie. They are not on any particular theological issue, but on the nature of tradition. The real division over men and women is to be found in whether the experience of the early church was normative, or just one era in church history. If the early church was the model for all time, women are inferior and that is that. If the church is still inspired by the Holy Spirit, we are capable of growth and capable of learning. If it is not then we should copy the experience of the early Christians, with all its mixtures of bizarre physiology, aspects of Roman inheritance law, shadows of Gnosticism, and honest attempts to live the gospel in a confused and confusing world. Which is what happens today, even in Sweden. Or perhaps we should say, especially in Sweden.

15

Cosmic Christ

'Caterpillars are not suffering to teach us something.' So writes Stephen Jay Gould, the Darwinian scholar. This argument comes from the view that God was kindly and put everything on earth for our benefit, and that animals led a happy life, and if lions swept down and killed deer, they only killed the weakest and sickest deer who were given a merciful end. Against this happy view, it was learned that a race of wasps laid their eggs in caterpillars, and the wasp larvae ate the caterpillars from the inside out, avoiding vital organs to keep their food supply fresh for as long as possible. This is scarcely a mercy killing. It is probably very painful, though supporters of the kindly God theory could speculate that caterpillars like being eaten, since the wasps inject some substance which causes the caterpillars to die in ecstasy. But that substance has never been found, and we are left with suffering caterpillars.

Gould rejects any meaning to this. This may be because he is left-wing in outlook, and remembers the social Darwinism in which dog-eat-dog was transferred from natural history to modern economics. It was argued that if creatures struggle for survival in biology they should do so in the marketplace. And he is surely right to be cautious in the face of constant attempts to find religious significance in some recent discovery or scientific theory which will soon be overtaken, or more often balanced, by another scientific discovery. And he is right to say that we should not assume that caterpillars only live for our moral instruction. They have their own lives and destinies. And those lives and destinies take in more than suffering, as do ours.

There have been other examples of such caution. Recently Stephen Hawking suggested that the a unified field theory in physics would lead to 'the ultimate triumph of human reason – for we should know the mind of God'. To which John Polking-horne replied, 'There is more to the mind of God than physics will ever disclose.' And when a recent set of astronomical observations indicated that the Big Bang theory of the formation of the universe was probably correct, newspaper reporters sought comments from various religious leaders. Of which the most appropriate came from someone who found the new discoveries 'interesting'. These things are interesting, and they should not be set aside, but they are only tiny parts of our lives and experiences.

Yet the creation cannot be ignored entirely. We may have to take on the whole destiny of a caterpillar, and every other living thing, and super-strings in physics and something else in microbiology. But if God made the world, and made it through Christ, then somewhere, somehow, the mark of Christ must be on it. And this is not all. If we were called upon to live the Christian life in a thoroughly alien world, in which there was nothing that was of God, or of Christ, then we would be right to leave this world as soon as we could. The Gnostic answer would be the right one. We would have no calling to do anything in this world, except to leave it. And we would have no calling to do anything with the people in this world, except to leave them. We would not belong in this world. We would have been dumped here through some accident, like travellers on a highway who have suffered a breakdown and found themselves in some strange territory of which they do not even know the name. Awaiting rescue, which is what some people think their real state is, and which is what some people think Christianity is, a sort of breakdown service to take them out of the world.

But human experience is that we belong in this world. Our bodies, and presumably our souls, are shaped for living in this world. Most people like the world, and most people like the people amongst whom they find themselves. If they object violently either to the environment in which they live, or to the people amongst whom they have to live, then this is evidence that they do not accept this as natural. Even the cynic who claims to expect everything to go wrong is usually enjoying it. And the very fact that we can be horrified by the thought of young wasp larvae eating the caterpillar from the inside out is evidence that this is not what we consider natural or right.

Early Christians appealed to science as they knew it, but they knew it as a branch of philosophy. It is philosophy which they discuss, and philosophy which stands for the caterpillar and the Big Bang and all the rest of it. And early Christian thinkers used philosophy and gave it their approval, even while they put it in a secondary position. It was not God, it was not the ultimate truth, but it led there. Origen and Augustine are the obvious examples, but there were two writers who went farther in the direction of claiming philosophy for Christ, and who did this, not incidentally, but as their main argument.

Justin Martyr was born in Palestine, probably into a Greek settler family, around the beginning of the second century. He was not a great thinker, but he was a seeker who had been instructed in all the schools of philosophy. He found them disappointing until he came to Platonism. This he took on board with enthusiasm, as a means of looking on God, the ultimate. He then met an old man in a field, who directed him to the Hebrew prophets who had foretold the Christ, and so he became a Christian. Around the year 150 he moved to Rome and wrote his *First Apology*.

'We have been taught that Christ is the first-born of God, and we have declared above that he is the Word of whom every race of men were partakers; and those who lived with reason are Christians, even though they were thought atheists, as, among the Greeks, Socrates and Heraclitus, and men like them ... Whatever things were rightly said among all teachers, are the property of us Christians ... For all the writers were able to see realities darkly through the sowing of the implanted word that was in them ... For the seed and imitation imparted according to capacity is one thing, and quite another is the thing itself ...'

Justin Martyr went on to write a *Second Apology*, and also the *Dialogue with Trypho the Jew*, before dying in the persecution of

Marcus Aurelius around the year 165. But for us his importance rests on his identification of the Christian life, and even the Christian name, with all those who have ever 'lived with reason', and who were able to 'see realities darkly'. He did this with Platonic teaching, shown when he made a distinction between the 'seed and imitation imparted according to capacity', and the 'thing itself'. And he was obliged to do this by the charge made against Christianity by its critics, that it had left the world on its own for thousands of years before the sending of Christ. Justin could have quoted the Bible to show that God had never left himself without witnesses, but he went further. All that lived with reason were Christians. Christ was active in them, even if they did not know it.

The second writer was Clement of Alexandria. Born around the year 150, he went to Alexandria and became head of the catechetical school, though he fled to avoid persecution in 202 and was succeeded by his pupil Origen. Clement was mainly concerned to counter the Gnostic threat, and saw Christianity as the true 'gnosis' or knowledge. But amongst his many writings are certain phrases about philosophy.

'Philosophy, then, before the coming of the Lord was necessary to the Greeks to bring them to righteousness, but now it is profitable to bring them to piety ... For God is the cause of all good things, but of some primarily, as of the old and new covenants, and of others consequentially, as of philosophy ... for philosophy educated the Greek world as the law did the Hebrews to bring them to Christ. Philosophy therefore is a preparation, making ready the way for him who is being perfected by Christ.'

And yet all this academic acceptance of philosophy and culture may have cut very little ice with the ordinary Christian who then, as now, grumbled that this was only confusing decent folk who believed without having to use all those complicated arguments. And who took philosophy to be so wrapped up in pagan religion it was dangerous to take it on board. And yet in the long run it was taken on board, and the pagans with it, though their religion was left behind.

And for our time the argument is not whether the mark of God is on the creation. This is usually admitted. The argument is more specific and more hysterical. Is there truth, or is there revelation, in other religions than Christianity? And to this the answer of the early church would have been thoroughly negative. The gods of antiquity were demons, and that was that. Of course there were good things in pagan thought, such as the growing belief in a single deity, and the idea that morality was demanded, but essentially other religions were bad. The worship of the sun may have been an exception, but if the sun was associated with Apollo it was not acceptable. Otherwise it was a sufficiently remote object of worship to be nearer philosophy than religion as then understood. And much of the growth of early Christianity may have been undertaken by pagans using sun-worship as stepping-stones across the waters to Christianity.

Yet the hysteria of our day is usually misplaced. It is assumed that there is a stark choice. Either all religions except Christianity are totally false, or all religions are equally true. To which the answer is that both these positions are wrong. All religions cannot be equally true, since they disagree on so many vital issues, and since some involve human sacrifices and worse. And all religions except Christianity cannot be totally false, since most religions, including Christianity, have certain common convictions. Furthermore, if the mark of God is on the creation, and religions are part of the creation, then the mark of God should be on them. It is hard to argue that they are exceptions, the only exceptions, to the conviction that God is still lord of all. It is hard to believe that God is at work in all we experience except when we take part in the highest and most generous of activities.

Karl Rahner, whom many regard to be the finest theologian of this century, and whom all regard as the most difficult theologian of this century, wrote on this matter with his usual obscurity. 'Valid and lawful religion does not mean man's own interpretation of human existence.' Instead, 'Valid and lawful religion for Christianity is rather God's action on men, God's free self-revelation by communicating himself to man.' But this 'began at some point in time', and 'has a temporal and spatial starting point' in Jesus Christ. But is that 'chronologically simultaneous for all people'? To this question, Rahner says, he will 'leave it an open question (at least in principle)', and he goes on to say that because God wills the salvation of all, 'every human being is really and truly exposed to the influence of divine, supernatural grace', and we cannot suppose that God means 'that nearly all men living outside the official and public Christianity are so evil and stubborn that the offer of supernatural grace ought not even to be made in fact in most cases'.

Which is what we would have thought in the first place, unless we really did believe that most of the human race 'was so evil and stubborn' that this is what God had to do. But some people do believe that most of the human race are beyond the power or desire of God to save them. It is such people that argue that there is nothing in non-Christian religions. It is not because they know anything of such religions, or those who live them, but because they have such a dim view of humanity, or such a weak view of God's love. And against them Rahner writes of 'the need of God which bursts open and redeems the false choice of man by overtaking it'. In other words, we should look at this from the standpoint of God, not of ourselves.

But there is one thing which is troubling in all this. The reference to time. It is sometimes argued that non-Christian religions are preparations for Christ, as were the Hebrew prophets or the Greek philosophers, but as soon as Christ came, they ceased to be good and became bad. Rahner's thought would overcome this absurdity by suggesting that for each person there was a different moment at which the claims of Christ become evident, and this is commonly held by others. But there is still an assumption of preparatory religious systems, and this rules out religions such as Islam which arose after Christianity. It is better to avoid too much talk of religions being valid until a particular point in somebody's life. It is possible to argue that Islam can deepen the religious life of someone who always has been Christian and who is blessed by kindly acts of Muslims. It is better to leave all this as an 'open question', even if we do not follow Rahner in saying that we do this 'at least in principle'.

But what we believe about non-Christian religions will depend on what we believe about the creation, for they are part of it. If we believe the world bears the mark of God, then all religions must do so. But we will only believe that the world bears the mark of God if we believe that God cares enough for us to put his mark on us and on his world. In the long run, it depends on the love of God.

16

Rome

'The early church did indeed know nothing of Roman primacy in practice, in the sense of Roman Catholic theology of the second millennium, but it was well acquainted with living forms of unity in the Universal Church ... Undoubtedly, in this sense, the priority of the Universal Church always preceded that of particular Churches.' So wrote Cardinal Ratzinger, Rome's guardian of the faith, in 1983.

That the early church knew nothing of Roman primacy in the modern sense should surprise nobody, though in fact it will surprise a great many. But the claim that there was a modern papacy in the early church could only be taken seriously if it was believed that no development in church life had or should have taken place. On which subject enough has been said already. But if John Henry Newman showed that development in the papacy was natural and right, and that it was no shame that the papacy of his day was not exactly like that of the early church, it is equally true that development in the past implies development in the future. If the pope stays as he is, then he is not the pope. The papacy must develop, or it is not the papacy. And there is plenty of room for development.

But Cardinal Ratzinger was really concerned with another question. Is the church essentially universal or local? In 1983 he was dealing with the Anglican idea of church structures in national synods, loosely linked with one another. Against this, Rome argued that the universal was basic and the local came second. In fact this had been necessary for the Second Vatican

Council in the 1960s to favour the idea of of a 'college' or society of bishops sharing rule of the church with the pope, but it was an argument which went much further back into history. And, however strongly Ratzinger and others might argue for the church as universal, history since the 1960s has not seen development of the college of bishops for the whole world. It has seen development of national conferences of bishops in Roman Catholicism worldwide. So the local has triumphed in the years since the proclamation of the universal.

But the Roman primacy can or could exist with either idea. If it is assumed that local churches are basic, then we either have the bishop's diocese as the essential unit, or we have the local congregation. The local congregation is the ideal for Baptist and Congregational churches, which believe that any structure above the local congregation is purely voluntary and preferably temporary. It is not really of the church. The Presbyterian ideal is rather different; it assumes that there is a regional presbytery to which ministers and ruling elders are sent, and there are other courts of wider jurisdiction. Yet authority gets weaker as it goes up, not stronger. Classical Presbyterianism is really more local than universal. But all these outlooks stem from the late mediaeval concentration on the mass and the local congregation in which that supreme Christian act occurred. A church too widespread for a single mass was relatively unimportant.

And Roman Catholicism saw its ministry in terms of the mass; priest (including bishop) and deacon and sub-deacon were the essential orders because that was what was needed for Solemn Mass. And yet each diocese was in a sense autonomous; it is striking to see how Pius IX, the nineteenth-century pope regarded as the great extender of papal power, stood back from interfering with bishops of other dioceses. In those days it was unusual for the pope to dissent from the suggested list of candidates prepared when a new bishop was needed, and that was where the state had no hand in the matter. But usually the state did have a hand; early in the last century the vast majority of Roman Catholic bishops were nominated by civil rulers, and the formal proclamation that the pope should do so only came in 1917. And state nominations of bishops still linger on in some countries.

This is important because state nomination is a relic of popular election. Which election now only exists for the Bishop of Rome himself. There the cardinals, who are the representatives of the Roman parishes, are the electors – even though in fact most cardinals are now at the opposite end of the world. But the swing to the idea of the universal church being basic has swung all other dioceses into dependence on the diocese of Rome, which is the only really ancient diocese left in Roman Catholicism. The trouble with modern Roman Catholicism is that it is not Roman enough. All dioceses should be like Rome.

Again, it must be noted that election by representatives of the parishes should be followed by consecration of the future pope as bishop. Anything else is ceremonial, such as handing him keys and perhaps, in this modern age, passwords to get into computer programmes. Karl Rahner has noted, and there are few things which Karl Rahner has not noted, that there is no sacramental act by which a pope becomes a pope. The sacramental act is that by which he becomes a bishop, and though in modern times the person elected is always bishop of somewhere else, so need not be consecrated, in theory that is what makes him pope. Like any bishop anywhere.

Next, was the pope important because he was Roman, or because he was a successor of Peter? Bishops of great centres naturally have great influence. The patriarchs of Constantinople are still leaders in the Orthodox world, even though the Christians of Constantinople have been ground down to almost nothing. And yet Constantinople owed much of its position to its being the New Rome, and Moscow owed much to being the Third Rome, and in Orthodoxy some borough of New York may yet figure as a Fourth Rome. And it is significant that Rome began to be an important Christian centre when it ceased to be a political centre. There seems to be some process whereby the dignity of a city continues, like the Cheshire cat's smile, when its power has gone, and the smile falls to a religious successor. (In what some would regard as moving from the sublime to the ridiculous, it may be argued that the Archbishop of Canterbury only started to be regarded as a world leader of Anglicanism when Britian ceased to matter in world affairs.)

What was Roman mattered even if there was no Peter. On the other hand, Peter and Paul almost certainly died at Rome, and on one occasion appeal was made to both as founders of the Roman church. But Peter meant more as he was in some sense a leader of the apostles, and there was a single verse in a gospel, in a time when single verses meant a lot, saying 'You are Peter and on this rock I shall build my church, and the gates of hell shall not prevail against it.' Which might mean infallibility.

Nobody can prove that any early Bishop of Rome claimed infallibility; there was no such thing to claim. In 1930 Cuthbert Butler wrote: 'We are not so sensitive or so exacting in this matter of infallibility as our forefathers were.' And, 'Nowadays Catholics have, for the most part, settled down into a middle position, and are prepared to accept as right and true a great body of teachings and judgments of the pope, without requiring to know that it is guaranteed infallible ...' Lastly, 'The difficulty lies in the idea of infallibility at all, rather than in the infallibility of the pope.' If infallibility can become less urgent between 1870, when it was proclaimed to be vital, and 1930, when Butler wrote, what differences can there be between the early centuries and 1870? Or between 1930 and today?

As for the Roman church itself, the first thing to remember about it is that it was not Roman. It was Greek. There is a famous story of Wilfred, the great Latinizer of the English church, who went to Rome and was a bit put out when the pope turned aside from Wilfred to converse with his advisors in Greek, which Wilfred did not know. But that was at the end of the seventh century, after a period when the Roman church had been mainly Latin. Originally it was very Greek, and we are told that it was a collection of immigrant groups, which made for division and also for emphasis on the need for unity. In the first century it was already attracting some prominent Romans, of whom the best known was Flavius Clemens, consul for the year 95, later executed for his faith, and whose wife gave the land for a Christian cemetery. The bishop of those years was a Clement who may have been a slave in Flavius Clemens' household. He wrote an epistle to the Corinthians, whose general behaviour was no better than it had been when Paul was obliged to do the same thing. Clement's house was apparently used as a church, though part later became a temple for an oriental mystery cult, and in the fourth century a basilica was built on the site. There is one there still.

One product of those days was the *Shepherd of Hermas*, written by one Hermas who may have lived in Clement's day but wrote somewhat later. It is partly a vision of an old woman representing the church, and a shepherd representing forgiveness, and its theme is that sins may be fogiven in the Christian life. Not surprisingly, it is weak on the Trinity, which had not yet been worked out. At the end of the second century came the Victor who was rebuked by Irenaeus for setting forth the claims of Rome, which had not been worked out either, and perhaps have not been worked out now. And in the third century came the famous Cornelius who succeeded the martyr Fabian, and whose moderate policy to those who had denied the faith was rejected by Novatius and his faction. And then came Constantine.

If there is no truth in the claim that Constantine gave rule in the West to the pope, and there is none, he did give successive popes a vacuum in which to expand. He did this by moving his centre to the East. And he spent a vast amount of money building churches in Rome, though he had to build them away from the centre in order not to offend the pagans. This was a great nuisance to the Christians who had long walks to take on a Sunday; of his ten new churches the cathedral of St John Lateran, which is still the cathedral though tourists do not know this, was extraordinarily large and expensive. It fell down in the ninth century, and has been rebuilt and falling down almost ever since.

Damasus was bishop from 366 until his death sixteen years later; a majority of clergy and laity elected Damasus in one place while a minority elected a rival in another place. Nor was that all, for 'blood ran in the streets' over this business, and the emperor had to intervene to restore order and banish Damasus' rival. This is worth remembering when we are told that state intervention in such affairs is an outrage. Apart from establishing his authority and building churches, Damasus is most famed for having sent Jerome to live in a cave at Bethlehem, which most Westerners felt the best place for him. This resulted in the Vulgate Latin translation of the Bible, Jerome's great accomplishment.

Another work of Damasus was to clean up the Catacombs, those underground burial chambers which still astonish the modern world. Since the very existence of an underground system running for hundreds of miles had been forgotten for centuries, their accidental discovery in 1578 led to all sorts of false notions. It was believed that they had been dug out as sand-pits and used later for Christian burials; in fact they were dug solely for burials. It was believed that they were used for regular worship by persecuted Christians; in fact almost the only worship which occurred was on the anniversaries of the dead in question. As Jerome wrote of his boyhood: 'Many a time did we go down into the catacombs. These are excavated deep in the earth, and contain, on either side as you enter, the bodies of the dead buried in the wall ... Only occasionally is light let in to mitigate the horror of the gloom, and then not so much through a window as through a hole. You take each step with caution ...' Along the corridors the dead lie in rows dug into each wall, 'like the berths in a ship'. Some graves have a small glass jar with what seems to have been dried wine, probably from the eucharist celebrated at the funeral.

Of course there was nothing secret about these burial places. You cannot bury six or seven million bodies in secret, and there was no reason for them to be secret. But why did the Christians of the second and third centuries devote such a vast amount of money to having these catacombs excavated? We know that by the middle of the fourth century burial in them was rare, and that after the sack of Rome in 410 there was not enough wealth for more digging, but why dig them in the first place? The answer probably lies in beliefs about the soul lying with the body, such as Origen denied. But it may have been merely a witness to the resurrection of the body before a world which denied this.

Two Roman bishops have been known as 'the great'. Leo was

pope from 440 to 461, and is surprising as not having known Greek. He threw his weight behind the orthodox party in the battle over the person of Christ, and in 452 he met Attila the Hun and persuaded him not to attack Rome. In fact Attila had pressing business elsewhere, but he did not attack Rome, and when the Vandals entered the city in 455 they were persuaded by Leo to limit their vandalism. Leo filled the vacuum left by the Roman empire, and by the new empire of Constantinople which was unable to do much more in Italy than keep the barbarians warlike by pinprick attacks.

Gregory the Great was pope from 590 until 604. Of wealthy origins, he was prefect of the city until 574 when he turned his home into the monastery of St Andrew, became a monk, represented the pope at Constantinople, returned as abbot, and was seized and dragged unwillingly to his consecration as bishop. He sent missionaries to Britain and elsewhere, and he organized religious life, promoted monastic houses, rooted out abuses, and everywhere demanded that the Roman church be regarded as 'the head of all the churches' through its foundation by Peter. He was the first pope to be a head of state and a clearly political figure, and if he rebuked the patriarch of Constantinople for claiming to be universal patriarch, his own claims were scarcely more modest. Having lived at Constantinople, he had no illusions about its capacity to be useful in the West.

Was Rome a good thing for the church? Perhaps yes, or perhaps not, and yet it could not be ignored. Christ took human nature in the Roman empire, and Roman soldiers put him to death. A Christianity which does not have some sort of theory about Rome is missing out on something significant. It is true that Latin is not as important in church or state or university as fifty years ago, and it is true that Rome is now a tourist nightmare. But history is history and if Christians other than Roman Catholics do not take Rome into account, then they are implying that history does not matter, and Christianity is not really the taking of flesh. How they should take it into account is another matter.

17

Constantine

'Constantine was a religious man with very precise beliefs, attitudes, and values. But these were most certainly not Christian.' So wrote Alistair Kee in 1982, arguing that 'The policy of successive pagan emperors had failed. They had tried to dam the river and it had engulfed them. What genius to reverse the policy and, purporting to assist the river in its course, actually to divert it along a newly prepared route!' And, as Constantine used Christianity in his drive to control the empire, 'Christianity was transformed.' The result has been that 'The protest against Constantinian Christianity has been preserved, therefore, in movements such as Marxism, which have had to develop outside religion, though they have been indebted to early Christianity.'

With some of this it would be hard to argue; Christianity was certainly transformed, though whether it thereby ceased to be Christianity is another matter. And whether it was altogether a bad thing is another matter. Even Professor Henry Chadwick, reviewing Dr Kee's book, agreed that Constantine saw God as a source of earthly success, 'and above all giver of victory on the battlefield. This God enabled him against all odds to liquidate successively superfluous colleagues ...' But he complains that Dr Kee 'deploys every conceivable argument ... to deny the emperor the last element of informed charcoal-burner's faith that Jesus Christ had been sent to a troubled world. Christ was his rival, not his saviour.'

There are two questions here. Was Constantine a Christian? Historians have generally agreed that he was. Jacob Burckhardt

130

did not; he said that because of his drive for power, he must have been 'essentially irreligious'. Yet he was much at his prayers, and it is hard to believe that this was entirely a sham. He was hesitant in matters of faith, while resolute and active in all things else. John Holland Smith has argued that he needed 'the moral strength that awareness of being "instinct with the divine" gives to the naturally religious mind'. He was a Christian, he was religious, and yet he was not a good Christian, which is quite another thing. After his death the Western church was careful not to make him a saint; if he was remembered with gratitude it was more for his rule than for his Christianity.

The other question is whether the church was or is of such a nature that a single lifespan could change it forever. Chadwick goes on to suggest that Kee's analysis is part of a tendency to suppose that there was the perfect early church once upon a time, and then the Constantinian church, which must be wiped out for the earlier one to be re-discovered. 'A radical Protestant or even mediaeval streak surfaces in occasional suggestions that Catholicism is a product of Constantinian political theory. Without it Kee feels that Christianity would not have developed its episcopal hierarchy ...' Is the church alive or is it dead? If alive, it can develop, rectify false steps in its life, and return always to the fount of its origin, guided by the Holy Spirit. If dead, it is just as twisted as Constantine or somebody else left it. Radical reformers blamed everything on Constantine. Later radicals blamed everything on the reformers. But if the church is not alive, then it is nothing. And the question of whether the church can recover from wounds is far more important than the question of whether Constantine wounded it.

As for the Constantine of history, he was born in the Balkans about the year 280, the son of Constantius, a military man who had made himself emperor. His mother Helena was long believed to be the daughter of Old King Cole. She was more likely a barmaid in what is now Turkey. Since Old King Cole first got into nursery rhymes as a cloth merchant and was not a king at all, she did not lose all that much by not being his daughter. As a boy Constantine lived as a virtual hostage in the eastern capital of the empire, from which he was given leave to join his father, or took leave to do so. With Constantius he crossed to Britain and when the father died at York in 306 the son was proclaimed 'augustus' by the army. There followed years of diplomacy (including a marriage to Fausta, daughter of one of his rivals) and years of wars and quiet murders before he was master of the empire, and the previous system of four rulers came to an end.

Much has been said of his having a vision of the cross before winning the battle of the Milvian Bridge which left the way open to Rome. There can be no doubt that he believed he saw such a vision when he spoke of it many years later, but in those days divine favours were regarded as present at every battle, and it is still doubtful if at that time he saw much difference between Christ and the unconquered sun. His final war was with Licinius, and this involved armies and navies such as the world would not see in another thousand years. Licinius surrendered on terms (he had been married to Constantine's half-sister) but was done away with nonetheless.

As an emperor, Constantine was a success. To quote Holland Smith again: 'He cared whether the people were fed. His tax demands were reasonable. He forced none into slave labour ... His people had nothing to fear from him, as long as they were loyal.' But if there was as much as a suspicion that they were not loyal, death was instant. In 326 he had his wife and a son by an earlier marriage, Crispus, put to death. All memory of them was wiped out. Of course he was not the first emperor to eliminate any possible danger to the well-being of the sixty or eighty million people in his care, and the appalling murders after his death were to show that he was not the last emperor to do so either. He may possibly have had a cruel streak, but he enjoyed administration more than murder. And if he guarded against threats from within, he also guarded against threats from without. His military policy, with the re-organization of the army into smaller units, kept the invaders at a distance. And to pay for this he created, perhaps the greatest achievement of all, a solid currency. It had been a long time since the Roman empire had known such peace and prosperity.

His religious policy was cautious. In 319 he visited Rome, would not sacrifice to Jupiter, and is said to have turned to the east when the offended citizens gave him a frosty reception. But he was turning east in any event, and the Balkan triangle was really the core of his empire. Only a very small proportion of the people were Christian; if they were a larger proportion in eastern towns, they were a smaller in western, and hardly to be found in rural areas. That being the case, Constantine needed the pagans and he may have originally thought that pagan gods were real, even if the Christian God was supreme. But whatever he thought, he was careful to build his vast churches well away from the pagan heart of the city of Rome, or the pagan heart of any other city. Pagans and Christians were to co-exist in the empire, and few pagans were persecuted. When they were, it was usually for involvement in witchcraft or sexual offences; Constantine had a horror of sexual irregularities. But if they were not per-secuted, their temples lost much of their wealth; the estab-lishment of a strong currency depended very largely on gold taken from temples.

In dealing with heresies he was unsuccessful, and there is no doubt that his practical turn of mind gave him little insight into theology. He was not the sort of man to worry overmuch about the origin of the soul. But having committed himself to the Christian faith, however gingerly, he could not allow Christians to be divided on critical matters with resulting danger for the empire. On Arianism he at first suppported what we now con-sider the orthodox party, though he repudiated the zealous work of his ultra-orthodox envoy in deposing all those thought to be Arian. At Nicaea he did not demand that a certain set of doctrines should be accepted, for he knew that he had only limited power in this area. But he put what weight he had behind what he thought was the most reasonable view, and the view most likely to succeed. When it turned out that the union at Nicaea was not as real as it had seemed at the time – had seemed both to him and to those who had new doubts when they got back home – he wavered, and then leaned a bit more to the Arians. It has been argued that he was influenced by the single entirely divine person of the Father in the Trinity as Arians saw it, which corresponded to the single emperor as he was himself. Perhaps so, but he was more likely to have tired of the orthodox party who could not bring unity, and hoped another approach would be more successful.

As for the Donatists, it is certainly true that he failed to bring peace, but it is not clear that anyone could have done any better. That he interfered cannot be charged; the Donatists had asked for his judgment, and they had rejected what was, on the face of it, a reasonable compromise. That the most ferocious measures were then employed against the Donatists is true, but they themselves were scarcely pacific, and peace and order were at stake. Perhaps some chance to bring peace was lost, but it is hard to say which chance.

When Constantine died in 337, after the baptism which had been so long delayed, he was laid to rest in the Church of the Apostles which he had built, surrounded by figures of the twelve as if he were Christ. This symbolized his real problem; how could he be a true Christian which demanded a rejection of any other god, and how could he at the same time be an emperor which demanded that he be divine? He did his best to be both at once, and even his dead body kept the problem alive. Fortunately the Church of the Apostles had been hastily built with materials removed from older buildings, as was the case in most of Constantine's building programmes. Very shortly after the emperor's body had been set in place, the building threatened to collapse on top of that body. It was therefore removed and the problem of whether a Christian emperor was also a Christ ceased to trouble the church. The danger was avoided with a little help from the construction industry.

Constantine was important to the church; that cannot be denied. Yet he did not and could not remake the church as if it were some sort of mechanical structure. As a living and changing and self-healing body, the church can never be post-Constantinian or post-Enlightenment or post-Structuralist or post anything else. Whatever is done to it, it is still the One, Holy, Catholic, and Apostolic Church. One Holy, Catholic, Apostolic, and Scruffy. Sometimes very scruffy. But still glorious.

Bibliography of Sources

Adams, Douglas, *Life, the Universe, and Everything*, Pan Books 1982

Blythe, Isobel, *A Study of Female Circumcision*, M.A. Dissertation, Glasgow 1984

Bonner, Gerald, *St Augustine of Hippo: Life and Controversies*, SCM Press 1963; revd edn The Canterbury Press 1986

Brown, Peter, *Augustine of Hippo: a Biography*, Faber & Faber 1967

Burckhardt, Jacob, *The Age of Constantine the Great*, Routledge & Kegan Paul 1964 (reprint)

Butler, Dom Cuthbert, *The Vatican Council 1869–1870*, Collins Fontana 1930

Chadwick, Henry, review of Alistair Kee's book in *The Times Literary Supplement* of 28 May 1982

Chadwick, Nora, *The Celts*, Penguin Books 1970

Crouzel, Henri, *Origen*, T. & T. Clark 1989

de Waal, Esther, *The Celtic Vision: Prayers and Blessings from the Outer Hebrides*, Darton, Longman & Todd 1988

Edwards, Ruth B., *The Case for Women's Ministry*, SPCK 1989

Ferguson, John, *Pelagius: A Historical and Theological Study*, Heffer 1956

Fox, Robin Lane, *Pagans and Christians*, Viking 1986

Gould, Stephen Jay, *Hen's Teeth and Horses' Toes*, Norton 1983

Hardy, Edward R., in Bruce, Michael, and Duffield, G.E., *Why Not? Priesthood and the Ministry of Women*, R.T.Beckwith/Manor Press, Abingdon 1976

Hawking, Stephen, *A Brief History of Time: from the Big Bang to Black Holes*, Bantam Press 1988

Jung, C.G., *Civilization in Transition*, Routledge & Kegan Paul 1964

Jungmann, J.A., *The Early Liturgy : To the Time of Gregory the Great*, Darton, Longman & Todd 1960

Kee, Alistair, *Constantine versus Christ : The Triumph of Ideology*, SCM Press 1982

Ker, Ian (ed.), *Newman the Theologian : A Reader*, Collins 1990

MacDougall, Hugh A., *Racial Myth in English History*, Harvest House, Montréal 1982

MacMullen, Ramsay, *Constantine*, Dial, New York 1969

MacMullen, Ramsay, *Christianizing the Roman Empire AD 100–400*, Yale, New Haven 1984

Nock, A.D., *Conversion: The Old and the New in Religion from Alexander the Great to Augustine of Hippo*, Clarendon Press 1933

Polkinghorne, John, *Reason and Reality: The Relation between Science and Theology*, SPCK 1991

Rahner, Karl, *Theological Investigations Vol XIV*, Darton, Longman & Todd 1976

Ratzinger, Joseph, 'Anglican-Catholic Dialogue: Its Problems and Hopes', *Insight*, Vol I, No III, March 1983

Rousselle, Aline, *Porneia : On Desire and the Body in Antiquity*, Blackwell 1988

Ruether, Rosemary Radford, in Loades, Ann (ed.), *Feminist Theology : A Reader*, SPCK 1990

Smith, John Holland, *Constantine the Great*, Scribner, New York 1971

Steinberg, Leo, *The Sexuality of Christ in Renaissance Art and in Modern Oblivion*, Faber & Faber 1984

Stevenson, J., *A New Eusebius*, SPCK 1957

Tavard, George H., *Women in Christian Tradition*, University of Notre Dame Press, Notre Dame 1973

Weil, Simone, *Waiting on God*, Routledge & Kegan Paul 1951

Williams, Rowan, *The Wound of Knowledge : Christian Spirituality from the New Testament to St John of the Cross*, Darton, Longman & Todd 1979